Kicking It

Kicking It:

THE NEW WAY TO STOP SMOKING PERMANENTLY

David L. Geisinger

Grove Press, Inc./New York

First Edition 1979
First Printing 1979
ISBN: 0-394-50291-4
Grove Press ISBN: 0-8021-0165-8
Library of Congress Catalog Card Number: 78-56045

Library of Congress Cataloging in Publication Data

Geisinger, David L
Kicking it.

1. Cigarette habit. 2. Behavior therapy.
I. Title.
RC567.G44 1979   362.2′9   78-56045
ISBN 0-394-50291-4

Manufactured in the United States of America

Distributed by Random House, Inc., New York

GROVE PRESS, INC., 196 West Houston Street, New York, N.Y. 10014

To Tillie, *my mother,*
my greatest teacher.

Contents

8 · Contents

ACKNOWLEDGMENTS

Many years ago Claude Steiner and I designed and worked together on a stop-smoking project which became the seed of this book. It may be a cliché, but nevertheless it is the simple truth that this book would never have been written without his loving support, encouragement, and wise counsel from the very beginning. He has been a political mentor, a dear friend, and a soul brother to me.

Thanks also to Elizabeth Tops for her early support and interest in this book; to Carmen Kerr for her valuable suggestions; to Bob Cantor for his tough and honest feedback; to Judith Bolker for her generous help with the referencing; to Betty Peskin, executive and organizer extraordinaire; to all my clients for their collective wisdom, particular contributions, and good wishes; to Alan Rinzler, my editor, for tightening the screws where they needed tightening and for having faith in the project when I brought it to him; to the Modern Jazz Quartet, whose delicate magic helped to keep the flow going while I wrote.

My special thanks to Evan Daniel Geisinger for his enthusiasm, his inventiveness, his sense of humor, and, most of all, his loving, patient self while his father was writing this book.

11

Introduction

by Claude M. Steiner, Ph.D.

It is a difficult thing for us to focus clearly on the fact that approximately 40 percent of the adults in this country are seriously addicted to a most damaging drug. Their addiction is overwhelming, expensive, the cause of many thousands of deaths each year, and the suspected cause of emotional problems as well. It is hard for us to see in clear perspective the vast, monstrous extent of the damage caused by this drug.

We tend to think of alcoholism as a serious problem; heroin and narcotic addiction bring fear to our hearts when we confront them. But the addiction to nicotine, to cigarette smoking, because of its very prevalence, is difficult to see in the same light.

If every other adult smokes, then surely this cannot be a serious addiction, we seem to reason. The fact that newspapers and billboards carry constant encouragement to smoke also leads us to believe that this is not a serious problem: how could anything so popular be really bad for us?

Smoking has been determined to be hazardous to your health, but surely it is not a *serious* hazard. Every serious

13

recent addiction—to tranquilizers, opiates, amphetamines, and barbiturates—has the same history. For years these substances were pursued by people who were being told not to worry about them, that they were safe and harmless. In many cases the users were told this by their own physicians, no less.

In time the danger from these drugs became clear. Tobacco alone has so far escaped this process. Why? Because the billions of dollars sunk into advertising by the tobacco companies have dulled our senses to the obvious.

None of the smoke screens, rationalizations, and evasions can dismiss this important fact: we are a nation of nicotine addicts.

Every smoker knows in his or her heart that there is something profoundly wrong with smoking. And I have encountered extremely few people who wouldn't give up cigarettes if only they could. This book is definitely written for them.

For every person who smokes in this country there are three others who don't. And a large majority of those who don't smoke are vitally concerned with the problem as well. Our children smoke, our parents smoke, our friends smoke, and we are worried about their health. People light up during a meal, or on the bus, and spoil our enjoyment of food, travel, and even the outdoors. Some of us are obliged to sit in smoke-filled rooms and inhale tobacco smoke, which we hate. This book is also for us.

Meanwhile, the tobacco companies in their callous search for new markets develop a never-ending number of new brands: natural cigarettes, long cigarettes, short cigarettes, cigarettes for women, cigarettes for blacks, and cigarettes for adolescents. Every new market is feverishly assaulted, and every potential smoker is relentlessly pursued.

At the same time large grass-roots movements and

organizations such as GASP and the American Cancer Society organize the fight against the killer weed. So far it is an uneven battle, but sanity is definitely gaining ground in the struggle. This book is part of that struggle.

The topic of smoking is clearly one of great importance to all of us, and this book is an intelligent, creative, thoughtful, and, above all, practical and useful contribution.

David Geisinger is a psychologist, a psychotherapist, and a behavioral scientist eminently qualified by his training and experience to deal with this problem. He and I conducted the first stop-smoking program in San Francisco in 1968 at the Center for Special Problems. We worked together on the pilot program, after which I went on to other matters. Dr. Geisinger continued his investigation and work with cigarette addiction. In the last ten years he has improved and expanded the method which we began. This book is the outcome of his work.

This is not just an extremely well-organized manual on how to stop smoking. It is that, but it is also a thorough analysis of what smoking is all about sociologically; what it has to do with the American way of life, corporate greed, advertising, and mass manipulation.

This book teaches the reader how to conquer the cigarette-smoking habit and gives hope that the national tide of cigarette addiction can be contained and turned around.

Any person or group of persons can sit down with this book and over a period of weeks systematically deal with and defeat their smoking habits.

One of the major reasons why the method presented here is so successful is that it involves a large number of habit-breaking techniques, each of which has its own separate effectiveness. These techniques have been carefully selected and put together in a unique, powerful program for stopping cigarette-smoking addiction.

While it is obvious that no system can be perfect, I have used this approach with my clients for years and am convinced that anyone who follows the instructions faithfully will succeed in kicking the habit.

If you are a smoker, this book is just for you.

Foreword

"Not to fall asleep is distinguished.
Everything else is mere popcorn."
—Saul Bellow, *Humboldt's Gift*

The smoking of tobacco probably originated among the Mayan civilization more than 500 years ago and then progressed northward through Central America, Mexico, and the rest of North America. Among these native cultures it was used principally in religious ceremonies.

When the Spaniards returned to their homeland after their voyages to the New World in the early sixteenth century they brought tobacco back with them in the form of cigars. At first these *cigarillos* were meant to be a luxury for the wealthy, but soon the beggars of Seville began to pick up the discarded butts and, wrapping them in paper, smoked them: the precursor of the cigarette had been created.

In the mid-1500s a French ambassador, Jean Nicot, introduced the weed to his country—the scientific term for tobacco, *Nicotiana tobaccum,* derives from his name—and later in that century Sir Walter Raleigh brought it back to England upon his return from North America.

Although cigarette production did not begin in the

17

United States until the 1850s, more than a billion cigarettes a year were being manufactured here by the end of the century. By the late 1970s well over 600 billion cigarettes were manufactured each year in the United States alone!

A brown plague was unleashed upon the world when tobacco was lifted from its religious context and restrictions upon its usage were removed, a plague that has contributed to the deaths of more people than the infamous black plague of the fourteenth century.

Cigarette smoking has probably caused more bodily harm than all the wars of recorded history combined. Over 80,000 people died in the United States of lung cancer alone last year. The major cause of lung cancer is cigarette smoking. It has been estimated that during the past ten years cigarette smoking was a causative factor in the deaths of at least 2 million Americans,[1] and countless numbers of people in other countries where cigarette smoking is commonplace. It has not merely reached epidemic proportions, it has become a scourge, a health disaster unparalleled in the history of the world.

Although smoking has always had its critics, the far-ranging and deadly serious consequences of habitual cigarette smoking did not really begin to make their impact on the public's attention until the *Surgeon General's Report on Smoking and Health* was published in the mid-1960s. It was only a few years after this report came out that I had an experience which kindled my interest in helping people to stop smoking.

A man had come to my office for an initial consultation. He was in his early sixties, he had lived most of his life in the Southwest, had been a Texas Ranger when he was younger,

---

1. Sidney S. Field, "Time to Crack the Cigarette Lobby," *Reader's Digest,* July 1976.

and later a sheriff. He had retired because of illness and hadn't worked for some time as a result of his disability.

During the hour that I interviewed him I gradually discovered that in the past ten years or so he had had two major heart attacks, one lung removed because of cancer, and emphysema in his remaining lung: heart disease, emphysema, and cancer—the three big ones. He was a walking medical disaster. As we spoke he chain-smoked cigarillos, inhaling every puff; he smoked four or five during the hour.

A very direct man, he asked, "Can you help me stop smoking?" He had smoked two or three packs a day since he was a young man.

I was a new therapist at the time. His request, accompanied by his furious smoking as he told me of his tragic medical history, so intimidated me that I told him I couldn't help him. If heart disease, cancer, and emphysema couldn't persuade him to stop, I thought, how could I?

I think of this man occasionally, wonder if he is still alive, and feel a sense of sadness and regret that we are not having our consultation now instead of then. Years of experience have taught me that once people have gotten over their embarrassment and made the decision to "go public" by asking for help, and once they have expended the time and energy to find a source of this help, they can be considered well on the way to their goals.

If you are a smoker, your decision to read this book is actually your request for help. I believe you'll find the help you need here, and a good deal of it, but I must tell you in advance that there are no miracle cures promised, and a fair amount of commitment and effort will be required of you.

No matter what your particular smoking or health history, you needn't be intimidated by it. I'd feel quite optimistic about your ability to quit smoking as long as you took your task seriously. I mean by this that for some time to come you should give the execution of this program a very high priority in your life and decide to stick with it even through what may be some difficult moments on the way to your goal.

I have tried to assure that the program described in this book is both a practical and a broad-ranging one. The techniques it makes use of are derived from a wide variety of sources; among them are behavior modification, hypnosis, transactional analysis, and certain consciousness-raising techniques, as well as several of my own invention.

It could easily be argued that there are as many different smoking patterns as there are smokers, yet somehow an effective program must encompass these differences and, in a way, transcend them. Whatever the differences, it is equally true that most of the fundamental aspects of cigarette smoking are strikingly similar from one person to another. I tried my best to take all these considerations into account.

This book was written both for people who have never made an attempt to quit before this one, as well as those who, for one reason or another, were not successful in previous attempts.

It has been my overriding concern that what is suggested here makes good common sense. If this sense is not always immediately obvious to you in the short run, I trust that it will become so in the long run. With respect to smoking, at least, the long run is what counts most: many people can stop smoking for a day or even a week or two, or a month or even a year, entirely on their own. *Staying stopped,* of course, is what matters, and this book was written with one guiding purpose in mind: to help you *permanently* break the cigarette-smoking habit. Permanently means *forever*—never to smoke again.

The program described here has evolved over many years

of work with smokers such as yourself, in groups at clinics as well as with individual clients in my practice. At times I have worked with people who came for the sole purpose of learning how to stop smoking; at other times learning how to stop smoking became the reasonable and necessary outgrowth of a more general psychotherapy, one concerned with the health of the whole person, the person as an ecological system. All the techniques have therefore been tried, either singly or in combination, with a large number of people, and in many instances the procedures have been modified and made more practical by the suggestions my clients made after following them.

It is not possible at this time for me to discuss this program from a formal scientific perspective, to present hard data demonstrating its efficacy. To gather these data would require a very complex research design, a large number of control groups, lots of time, equipment, personnel, money— and, of course, the inclination to conduct such an investigation. I have had neither the time, equipment, personnel, money, nor, to be quite frank, have I had the inclination to gather these and perform the research.[2]

I am inclined to believe that stopping smoking is very much a personal matter for each one of us. Ultimately, it rests upon a quiet and private decision we make deep within ourselves. Nothing can happen without that decision (and I know that if you reflect for a moment on what I am saying here you understand just what I mean)—not even the most advanced, brilliantly conceived program will work—but everything can happen with it. We each come to that

2. D. L. Geisinger, "A Broad-Range Program to Eliminate Cigarette Smoking," in *Counseling Methods,* ed. J. D. Krumboltz and C. E. Thoresen (New York: Holt, Rinehart and Winston, 1976). (The differences between the pilot project described in this paper and the program in this book are great; comparisons between the two are not particularly meaningful.)

decision in our own way, for our own reasons, and at our own time.

I hope you have made the decision I am referring to by now, but if not I hope you will take the time *now* to do so. Once you've made that decision you are ready to use this book in order to implement it.

There is no time like the present to start saving your own life.

There are few simple solutions to any human dilemma including the one of how to break the smoking habit. The comprehensiveness of this program reflects the complexity of the problem we are dealing with. In a very real sense there is no simple "cure" for cigarette smoking; it is not a disease, not an affliction visited upon you. It is a psychological, physiological, social, and even political problem. You cannot simply have a technique or two applied to yourself and expect to be cured of a habit, especially an addictive one such as smoking cigarettes. It is unlike, for example, a bacterial infection which can be eliminated by the administration of the correct antibiotic, and which does not necessarily require your continuing attention and cooperation in order for it to work.

The elimination of a habit demands more of one, and so this program will demand more of you.

I am a psychotherapist by profession, and I have tried to make this book a *therapy* for eliminating the smoking habit. It is not simply a how-to-do-it manual, not just a collection of techniques. Like all therapies, it represents a particular point of view.

As I see it, therapy is basically a form of education (which is why I chose to title the chapters as I did). A quality education not only takes time but also requires, among other things, a personal interest in the material to be learned, a cooperative and trusting relationship between the student and the teacher, and a desire to learn—an openness to the process of change, for all learning is about change and involves changing. And, of course, there is no real change without work, without the expenditure of energy in the form of practice, perseverance, and discipline against some resistance, whether that resistance is internal or external to yourself—or both.

But effort is not all. There is a unique joy to be found in working well on something as meaningful and personally relevant as stopping smoking.

Before you begin the program itself, therefore, I ask that you reflect on your seriousness of purpose and your willingness to take on the project and its work at this time. If you are looking for a magical cure-all you will not find it here, but the magic of change surely can be yours if you will agree to enter into a cooperative partnership with me and the material contained in the chapters that follow. This program will work for you if *you* will work for you.

As with any program for change, there are literally thousands of ways to cut corners, to avoid or alter one thing or another. The more committed you are—the more serious of purpose you are—the fewer corners you will cut. I mean by this in particular that the exercises are meant to be done *quite literally,* just as they are described. For example, if the exercise is to imagine a certain scene for two 5-minute periods each day, it does not mean that you are to do this only if you can find the time. It means you must *make* the time—and "5 minutes" does not mean 2 minutes, and "twice a day" means just that. If you do it only once a day, you have cut a corner.

Bear this observation in mind: *the sooner you begin cutting corners, the more corners you will cut. The more corners you cut, the more you cut into your chances for success.* The decision rests with you alone: the greater your diligence, the greater the likelihood that you will reach your goal.

A few words are in order about some of the idiosyncrasies of this system of kicking the smoking habit. Among other things, you will discover a strong emphasis throughout the book on the analysis of cigarette advertising. At first this may seem somewhat irrelevant or even excessive to you. I ask that you bear with me and that you reserve judgment as to its relevance until you have fully completed the program. The discussion of advertising is one of those matters I referred to earlier whose relevance may not be immediately apparent to you. It will, I believe, become clearer as you progress from week to week, and I hope and expect that its beneficial influence will continue long after you have completed the formal part of this program, five or six weeks from now.

You may not be *aware* of being influenced by the ads you see on billboards or in newspapers or magazines, but I assure you that you *are* definitely being influenced by them. They affect you in subtle ways, keeping your smoking habit alive, stimulating your desire for a cigarette, increasing the likelihood that you will remain a smoker. Perhaps a dozen or more of these boosters to smoking are taken in by your eyes and impinge upon your consciousness every day. They not only influence established smokers to keep on the smoking path, they also help influence nonsmokers to start smoking. The recent and alarming growth in the number of women and adolescents who smoke can, I think, be almost wholly accounted for by advertising campaigns directed against them.

It is not really possible to understand the extraordinary pervasiveness of the cigarette smoking habit without a serious consideration of the influence of advertising. In fact, I believe that if the advertising of cigarettes were to be eliminated entirely and if the government simultaneously adopted a vigorous antismoking, public health advertising campaign, after several years the decline in cigarette smoking among the population would be dramatic. If this policy were continued, within a decade or so the number of smokers in the population would be a fraction of what it is today, and, of course, the death rate from smoking-related diseases would be markedly reduced.

Any smoking program that does not attend to this issue is simply missing the boat.

As the weeks pass and you follow the program carefully, you will gradually develop a new and very useful habit. All those cigarette ads that have been encouraging you to continue to smoke will eventually be transformed into allies strengthening your commitment to *stop smoking*. The ads will become opportunities, reminders to quit and stay quit, to keep the decision to quit in your consciousness. In effect, you are going to use the ads in an entirely new way, a way which is the exact opposite of what the cigarette manufacturers intended when they designed them. You are going to co-opt the ads and use them for your own healthy purposes. The way you are to accomplish this feat will become clear as you progress in the book.

To answer what might be your first question: yes, I was a smoker myself. I stopped several years ago—finally.

I began to smoke when I was a young boy, perhaps twelve years old. In those days, since I couldn't buy my own cigarettes, I would sneak the butts my father left in the ashtrays and smoke them in the bathroom in front of the mirror, trying to look very debonair, sexy, grown-up, and sophisticated, as the ads suggested.

My friends and I would even pick up butts from the street (just as the beggars of Seville did 400 years earlier) and smoke them while walking on the beach or on the roofs of the buildings in which we lived, or in the darkened balcony of the local movie theater. We discovered that people threw away big butts at bus stops—sometimes nearly whole cigarettes—because the bus would often arrive just after someone lit up, and passengers weren't permitted to smoke.

By the time I was fifteen or sixteen I was smoking regularly, a few cigarettes a day in the bathroom at school or in the house of a friend whose parents were more permissive than mine were (my father smoked, but he was damned if I was going to!). I gradually worked my way up the smoking ladder, just as you did, until I was smoking about a pack a day. I smoked this way for close to fifteen years before I gave it up.

In anticipation of your second question, I want to make it very clear that I really didn't *feel* like giving up smoking when I gave it up. I enjoyed cigarettes, a good deal in fact. To the best of my knowledge, at the time I stopped I wasn't suffering any ill effects from smoking other than an occasional mild morning cough and perhaps a slight increase in phlegm; I hardly noticed these.

I gave up smoking even though much of me didn't really want to. For me it was a moderately difficult struggle, but I knew there was no choice if I believed, as I did and do, in preserving my life and health, not in destroying it or reducing it wantonly. For some people it will be easier, for some it will be harder than it was for me.

Cigarette smoke is poison. No ifs, ands, or buts about it. The subject isn't open to question any longer.

If you smoke you are committing a form of slow suicide. Period. You are increasing the chances of illness for yourself and others around you. Period again.

Why continue? This is the third and most important question, one that only you can answer for yourself.

In a short time you can be a nonsmoker again, as you once were.

Do you remember that time? You didn't have the constant worry in the back of your mind that you were endangering your health or the health of your children or the health of others around you; it was much easier to exercise without finding yourself out of breath; your mouth tasted fresher and food was tastier; your sense of smell was sharper. You were free of all the other inconveniences of being a smoker, such as the increased danger of fire, minor damage to your clothing from a hot ash occasionally falling on them, the stale smell of tobacco smoke permeating your clothing and your hair and your hands, nonsmokers asking you to please move or put out your cigarette, having to move to a nonsmoking area of the library or theater or restaurant you're visiting, concerning yourself with whether you have enough cigarettes to last you through the meeting you're attending or whether you have enough cigarettes at home to keep you from having to make a late-night "cigarette run," or having to clear your throat dozens of times a day.

It will be a blessed relief to be a nonsmoker again. But you probably won't be so blessed for some time to come, so gear up and prepare to begin. We'll be off to a slow start and, as you gain confidence, we will pick up speed along the way.

This program has been designed so that you can do it alone and entirely at your own convenience. However, if you know someone else who wants to stop smoking and with whom you'd like to work in tandem or in a group, by all means do so. For many people, working with others on a project such as this is more fun, easier, more powerful, or more rewarding. Suit yourself; the program lends itself to both approaches equally well.

It is important that you read this book only *one chapter each week,* no more and no less; that's the way the program was designed. This short book, which you might normally finish in only a few hours, should, therefore, take you five or six weeks to complete. Do not read any chapter in advance. If you do, you will be cutting a corner and undermining your chances for success. Be patient.

Each chapter will conclude with an "Exercises" section which describes the weekly prescription for change. *There is no change without work, so you must do the exercises precisely and diligently.* A program of this sort requires a fair amount of attention to detail. Don't hesitate to reread any part of it that you need to in order to imprint it more firmly on your mind. Any additional effort you make will be repaid over and over again. As you read this book you will notice that it is somewhat repetitive in places. Bear with it—the repetition is there for a purpose. The learning of complex skills requires practice and all practice is a form of repetition: it is an essential part of the learning process.

Some people who pick up this book may still be uncertain whether they want to take up the project of habit breaking at this time, may need a bit of additional clarification or encouragement to help them decide. If you are in this category, I believe reading this book will help to make your decision easier. I hope it will encourage you to make a commitment to quit now.

Think about what you've read, discuss it with others if you care to, give it the attention it deserves, and remember what is at stake. Why have you chosen to kick the habit? How important is it to you that you do so? What priority will you give the matter of becoming a nonsmoker?

If by chance you are not a smoker yourself but are the friend or loved one of a smoker, you will find much here that can be useful in helping that person to quit.

The program in this book is your instrument of change, but only you can be the agent of that change, your own change as you start becoming a nonsmoker again.

Remember: THE SOONER YOU BEGIN CUTTING CORNERS, THE MORE CORNERS YOU WILL CUT. THE MORE CORNERS YOU CUT, THE MORE YOU CUT INTO YOUR CHANCES FOR SUCCESS.

1

Fresh(wo)man

Openers. You'll be starting off slowly and picking up momentum along the way, especially in the weeks following this one, so be patient. This chapter will introduce you to certain concepts and techniques that will set the stage for the most effective use of the program as it is presented in the following chapters. No matter how much you're "chafing at the bit," don't rush ahead or alter the sequence. Remember, the material in each chapter is meant to be "lived with" and worked on for a full week before the next chapter is read and applied.

Cooperating with Your Own Best Interests

Let's face it: more often than not, stopping smoking is a difficult business and the quitting process is seldom contemplated with pleasure. Some part of you probably wants to stop and another part of you just as likely doesn't. Nearly everyone who's been hooked on the smoking habit has felt this ambivalence.

If you're like most people, you've wished that you could somehow—magically—be rid of the habit without having to do a lot of work and without having to go through the withdrawal period. You visualize the miseries of withdrawal and you cringe. You recall with dread the stories you've heard about people practically "crawling the walls" or becoming impossible to live with while they were kicking the habit. You may even have crawled a few walls yourself if you've made attempts to quit before.

I wish I could promise you an easy time, but I can't. Nor can I be sure that it will be particularly difficult for you to quit. Even though this program has been expressly designed to make quitting as easy as possible, you may still find yourself crawling a wall or two or being an occasional grouch in contrast to your usual sweet self. It may be tough going for a while—or it may not be. There's just no way of knowing in advance, not even on the basis of your own past experience. This is an entirely new ballgame, so forget about making predictions about the future and stay here, in the present.

Logically, it could be argued that if quitting were going to be easy, you would have done it by now and wouldn't need the help of this book. But life situations change, people change in ways they aren't even aware of; logic and predictability are defied all the time.

This may be your time. Most importantly, you can and you should *make* it your time. Your own attitude is all important here: if you truly want to stop smoking you will relate to the material in this book *cooperatively*, with a spirit of openness to change, to giving it all you have and helping it work for you. If you relate to the material antagonistically, with a chip-on-the-shoulder attitude, I can promise you that you will handily defeat the program—it takes no genius to manage that—and defeat yourself in the process. Some people actually seem to enjoy this cutting-off-my-nose-to-spite-my-face position and later may even take some perverse pleasure in bragging to others about how "my habit is so strong that even Geisinger's program didn't work."

Enough said. If you are approaching the task ahead of you cooperatively, you stand a very good chance of succeeding. If you are approaching it antagonistically, you stand virtually no chance at all. Which side are you on?

Self-Deceptions and How to Counter Them

When you come right down to it, it isn't really that easy to remain a smoker these days. We're continually being told of new discoveries about the negative effects of smoking on health and we never hear anything to the contrary. Sure, representatives of the cigarette companies occasionally are heard to say that the fact that cigarette smoking causes disease is still not proven, but their arguments are so feeble and so obviously biased that it is hard for anyone to take them seriously. Even smokers who are desperate to hear anything that might allow them to feel a bit more comfortable about continuing to smoke have a hard time believing them: you can clutch at straws but you just can't hold on to hot air.

Most, if not all, people who continue to smoke know full well the harm they are doing themselves. In order to continue to smoke, therefore, these people must resort to various psychological maneuvers, clever attempts to justify or blot out the basic and unpleasant truth about smoking and health.

Rationalizations are the most common of these maneuvers. A rationalization is an excuse, an attempt to make something that is *not* reasonable *seem* as if it *is* reasonable. But no matter how you slice them, they're still baloney. There is just no way you can continue to smoke without using these forms of self-deception, though it is possible to block any awareness that you're doing so.[1]

Even though you have already begun this book, have chosen to embark on this program, you are no doubt still using these maneuvers. It is simply not possible to go through an exhaustive list of all the blarney smokers tell themselves—that would take a book in itself—so don't hesitate to add your own examples to those I am going to discuss here. It may take a bit of courageous and careful self-examination and self-confrontation on your part in order to do so, but it is a necessary first step. Rationalizations have a way of cropping up again and again and undermining your progress, so it is clear that you will need to sharpen your ability to recognize these lies that pass as truths before you can take measures to eliminate their pernicious influence upon you.

SIX BASIC RATIONALIZATIONS

Let's examine some of the most frequently used rationalizations and see how they work. Remember, these can occur at any time during the duration of the program and tend to be more common a bit later on, but forewarned is forearmed. Keep on the alert for them.

1. *"I don't smoke enough to harm myself."* If you smoke at all you are causing yourself harm, since the human body was not designed to have its insides polluted with the components of smoke. If you smoke a little, you do a little less harm to yourself than if you smoke a lot. You cannot smoke and do *no* harm. Therefore, why do *any* harm? It is your body; do it

---

1. One of the central components of *all* rationalizations is: do not recognize this as a rationalization; see it as though it is perfectly logical, perfectly reasonable; see it as though it makes simple common sense.

good. It is enough that smog and atmospheric pollution may contaminate the air you breathe and do you harm. Don't add to the problem!

2. *"Oh, what the hell . . ."* or, *"If it's not one thing, it's another."* People who use this rationalization pull the wool over their own eyes by telling themselves that cigarettes are only an insignificant danger in an already dangerous world. They say, in effect, "Oh, what the hell . . . people in my family die early anyway," or, "I could get killed in a car wreck just as easily as I could get cancer," or, "They're polluting the atmosphere so badly that smoking cigarettes won't increase the damage to my lungs," or, "Smoking is one of the few pleasures (!) I allow myself," etc., etc. Although we are all going to die sooner or later from one thing or another, it doesn't make much sense to step up the process or increase the likelihood of premature illness and death. As for giving you pleasure, if you have too few healthy sources of pleasure you ought to give some serious thought to figuring out why this is the case, and begin to work on changing the situation. The fact that many people have come to associate cigarettes with pleasure is related to the next rationalization.

3. *"Cigarettes relax me."* In truth, cigarettes are not capable of relaxing anyone—they have the opposite effect on your bodily processes. What actually relaxes you are the other things you do *while you happen to be smoking:* slowing down, sitting down, digesting a meal, pausing, taking deep rhythmic breaths (but of dense, poisonous smoke!), and other forms of relaxation and diversion. The cigarette manufacturers want you to develop this association of relaxation with smoking; it is one of the most fundamental ways of hooking you. You certainly can learn to relax better without smoking a cigarette which contains chemicals that artificially and harmfully alter your bodily processes. Later

we will use deep breathing and relaxation exercises to help you to feel calm and relaxed in a healthy way.

But there are many ways of reducing anxiety or tension in addition to these, ways that are convenient, effective, and simple, that make use of some of the elements of cigarette smoking without your having to smoke, without endangering your health. You will be finding out about these "allies" in later chapters, especially in Chapter 3, so that you will be able to switch over to them, if you need to, as you switch off cigarettes. You will be using these allies either singly or in combination with each other. Plenty of help will be available; your job will be to make full use of what is suggested.

4. *"Cigarettes pep me up."* Though nicotine is a stimulant, it is one only temporarily. Eventually, as a smoker you receive less vital oxygen as you breathe. The membranes in the air sacs of your lungs get clogged with the by-products of smoking, carbon monoxide, and other harmful gases reduce your oxygen supply and cause your overall energy level to drop. If you feel that you need a stimulant, try getting more sleep and/or increasing your oxygen supply by opening the windows; exercise—do some calisthenics, jog in place, dance. If it is simply not practical or possible to use any of these alternatives (if, for instance, you're in a classroom, or a business meeting, or if you slept poorly the night before), remember that you can always do a few minutes of deep breathing. This will freshen you, wake you up for a while, until either the situation changes, or you get your "second wind," or, if you can manage it, you have a chance for either a cat nap or sleep. A cup of coffee or tea can help if it is available. The point is that there are *always* alternatives to smoking a cigarette, no matter what purpose you've been having cigarettes serve. Try to see cigarette-linked situations as opportunities to come up with these alternatives, as challenges to your creative imagination. There is *absolutely no* problem or

circumstance which does not have a healthier and *more effective* solution to it than smoking a cigarette, *absolutely none*. Find these new solutions for yourself in addition to using the ones suggested in this book.

5. *"I'll gain too much weight if I stop smoking, and I'd rather be thin than . . ."* (*"not get cancer or emphysema"?!*) As usual, there are major flaws in this excuse. Studies have shown that the average weight gain for people who stop smoking is usually less than 5 pounds (one recent survey reported a figure of only 3½ pounds). Remember, this is an average figure; you may be among those who will gain less weight or no weight at all. Weight gain does *not* automatically occur when you stop smoking—not by any means.

Cigarette smoking is used by many people to occupy their hands or mouths when they are bored or tense or emotionally off-center in some other way. This kind of routine physical activity is temporarily distracting, enabling the person to blot out the unsettling state for a few minutes. Since eating is also an activity which occupies the hands and mouth for a period of time, it is easy to see how it can become a replacement for smoking.

In my work with smokers, I've found that it is mainly the occupation of the mouth and hands and *not* the actual ingestion of food that is being substituted when certain people increase their food consumption during the process of becoming a nonsmoker. It is the activity involved in the act of eating rather than the feeling of food in the stomach that is the important factor. Not realizing this, some people eat more food than is usual for them during this time because they have associated this busy-ness of the mouth and hands only with eating (and perhaps drinking) and smoking. But, of course, there are convenient noncaloric ways of occupying one's mouth and hands.

In the third chapter, when you have decisively begun to

cut back on cigarettes, you will be told about how to take care of these manual and oral components of the smoking habit without having to resort to eating more than you normally do.

In the meantime, you will be keeping a weight chart, described more fully in the "Exercises" section of this chapter, so that you can have an objective record of your weight and not have your mind play tricks on you, scaring you into using the rationalization that you must smoke in order to keep your weight down, a very common rationalization indeed.

Don't be fooled; there is no *valid reason* for having to choose between your "normal" weight and not smoking. You can be your "normal" weight *and* a nonsmoker as well. I put "normal" in quotes because, if you have been a smoker for many years, it is conceivable that the weight you have been is *less* than your healthy "normal" weight by several pounds. The chemicals in cigarettes can act as an appetite suppressant, though obviously not a very good one: there are millions of smokers who are substantially overweight.

This program is very mindful of the weight-gain issue. As you progress through the book you will come upon a number of techniques which will have a positive effect in reducing or eliminating the underlying causes of excessive weight gain after stopping smoking. Substitute forms of oral or manual activity, increased physical exercise, and ways of reducing tension are some of the specific treatments that will be described, and they will be relevant and useful whether or not you are concerned about weight gain.

Remember, *not everyone* gains weight after stopping smoking. But if weight gain happens to be one of your concerns, you might give some thought to this: it has been estimated that smoking one pack of cigarettes a day has the taxing effect on your heart equivalent to being *90 pounds overweight!*

Consider this startling figure for a moment. From the standpoint of overall general health—something of serious concern to you (if you aren't concerned about your health, why are you reading this book, why are you involving yourself in this program?)—the idea that you are better off being a smoker than having to contend with the *possibility* of a weight gain of several pounds is untenable, to say the least.

6. *"I don't have the will power."* As if there were a gene for "will power"—some people were born with it and some weren't! Will power is not something you are born with; it is something you can alter, develop, be taught. If you somehow think that you "don't have any will power," it is because you have been *taught* to believe that, and you are probably continuing to *teach yourself* this idea in ways you are not aware of . . . yet.

If you examine your life you will discover many instances where you use your "will power" quite effectively, whether it is in getting up in the morning to go to work though you still feel tired, or doing a routine errand that you'd rather not have to do. Why not in stopping smoking? More important, however, is that the concept of will power is rather useless for our purposes. It is usually based upon circular reasoning: if we do something we set out to do, we say we have "will power," and if we don't, we say we have "no will power." The program actually will be training you to strengthen your ability to choose for yourself the path you'd like to follow and to stay on it. That is what "will power" is all about.

By following the approach described in this book you will discover that you have all the "will power" that you need to stop smoking. You will certainly increase your power over this ridiculous habit if you follow the procedures discussed in this and the following chapters.

A FURTHER LOOK AT RATIONALIZATION

When you combine the increased risk of such things as heart and vascular disease, emphysema, and cancer, not to mention the host of other disease processes and health problems that smokers are more prone to get, you can't help but conclude that in order to smoke, *every smoker* without exception must be using rationalizations in order to keep smoking.

It takes courage to admit that these "perfectly reasonable" justifications for smoking are only clever untruths. It takes courage to admit to yourself that you have been and are rationalizing, though once you admit it to yourself it is much easier to admit it to others, and once you admit it to others it is much easier to stop rationalizing altogether. Once you stop your rationalizations you are considerably closer to being a nonsmoker, to being free of the habit. You really can't fully be a nonsmoker until you are no longer using rationalizations about smoking at all. This means that you have arrived at the point that no matter what your life situation, no matter what the extenuating circumstances, there can be no justification for smoking a cigarette.

Some common rationalizations used most often by smokers who really haven't committed themselves to quitting yet are as follows:

• "You can't teach an old dog new tricks; I've been smoking too long to stop."

• "I don't *really* want to stop just yet. I'll wait for the 'right' time."

• "They haven't definitely proven that cigarette smoking causes cancer or heart disease."

• "My Uncle Abner smoked for most of his life, and *he* lived to be ninety-one."

Do any of these sound familiar? In each case, *now,* uncover the faulty reasoning upon which it is based. *Now.*

Once you've begun a program of stopping, however, the rationalizations you are most likely to use will change. There are four rationalizations most common to smokers in this category, the category you are in. As we saw when we examined the rationalization about overeating, some people actually will have a problem in one or more of these areas. Yet as I said before, because these problems are almost always temporary, are never as injurious to you as smoking, and can all be dealt with and resolved by alternative approaches (approaches which are provided at various points in the program), they ultimately prove to be classic rationalizations.

These four most common rationalizations, all of which are based on fears, are: "If I stop smoking I'll . . .

1. gain too much weight."
2. have too little energy."
3. have trouble sleeping."
4. become nervous or grouchy or depressed."

Are there any others that you've used that aren't on this list? Before you read any further, stop and consider which rationalizations you've used or still use. What have you told yourself that has allowed you to continue smoking even though a part of you wanted to stop? Write these down now and reflect on them. Many suggestions will be offered for dealing with the major rationalizations as you progress in the program, but you should be thinking of your own creative solutions in addition to the ones described in this book. There is *always* a better solution than smoking a cigarette.

Speaking of rationalizations, I thought, naively, that I had heard them all. Recently, however, I met someone who had been involved for some time in experiencing one after another of the various new therapies that have sprung up around the human-potential movement. He believed that he had benefited in many ways from his experiences, but I knew that he had a long way to go if he could tell me, after I asked him why he still smoked, that "Cigarettes won't harm me because I can control their effect on me; it's a matter of mind over matter." He had stopped using his mind and it didn't seem to matter. There was no way he was willing to see that he was rationalizing; he was so intent on having his mind observe and control his body that he had stopped having his mind observe itself. In effect, no one was minding the mind and it slipped a rationalization through.

Rationalizations about smoking occur when you stop observing and analyzing the way you think, when you assume that you've found any way around the simple, inevitable truth: cigarette smoking is *always* harmful to your health and it always will be, no matter which cigarette you smoke, no matter what modifications cigarette technology comes up with, no matter how you choose to smoke. If you smoke at all, the only question is just how much harm you are causing to your health and to the general ecology, and this question is impossible to answer with any accuracy except by saying, "Any harm is too much harm."

The Influence of Advertising

All advertising for cigarettes is based upon one lie or another. Since an ad telling the simple truth about cigarettes would only discourage people from smoking, every ad campaign involves an often elaborate and sometimes subtle departure from the truth.

Reading cigarette ads, therefore, is like being given a

series of lessons on how to deceive yourself. These lessons, this perverse education, are going on whether you know it or not, and they are influencing you to act against your own best interests. Ads affect you if you only casually glance at them from time to time, as I indicated in the Foreword. Ads keep the momentum of your smoking habit from diminishing. They keep stimulating you to smoke another cigarette.

THE UNMASKING PROCESS

The only effective way to counteract this destructive influence is to analyze the components of the ads and "unmask" them. You may think that you can simply ignore them, but unfortunately this is probably not true. Ads can and do influence you even when you are not aware that they are doing so. Unmasking is the process of exposing the lies beneath the ads' surface so that the hidden truth in them is revealed in a way that will actually lend support to your quitting instead of encouraging you to continue smoking. It's the last thing the cigarette manufacturers would want you to do, so it *must* be on the right track.

Unmasking is a crucial part of the quitting process, and you will be actively involved in it throughout the course of this program. It will be an ongoing supplement to the other techniques for quitting that you will be learning as you proceed.

There are three major components of cigarette ads that we will be unmasking as we go along: the text or copy of the ads, the naming of the cigarettes themselves, and the visual images accompanying the text.

UNMASKING ADS: THE TEXT

Recently a particularly malicious form of trickery has begun to appear in advertising copy which makes abundant use of rationalizations as it goes about trying to maneuver you psychologically.

The ad says, in a tone of "genuine" warmth and sympathy (which so cleverly appeals to all your own harmful rationalizations), that if you are one of those who are not convinced in the "controversy" about whether or not smoking is bad for your health (as if there is any reasonable controversy at all!), and if you are one of those people who have tried and have just not been able to stop (nearly everyone who smokes, or who has smoked, fits into this category), or who just "plain likes to smoke" (this provides you with a rationalization in case you can't come up with enough of your own), you can always smoke "Slicks" because they have low tar and nicotine (and this is meant to imply that you can smoke them without doing yourself harm!).

Let's begin the unmasking with Vantage [(Disad)-Vantage]. Here is a cigarette that makes use of a welter of sly techniques in its ads, as the following excerpt clearly demonstrates. On the left side of the page you will read selected quotes from a recent ad, and on the right side is the unmasking or debunking of each selection.

In this particular double-page ad there are four boxes arranged along the top of the paper with a column of copy beneath each of them.

The first box is headed, "If you smoke."

Ad Copy	Unmasking
We're not telling you anything you don't know when we acknowledge that a controversy about smoking exists.	Controversy, my foot! Sounds real big of them as they begin by soft-pedaling and buttering you up. But the ad starts with a lie: there is no controversy! As it says on every pack of cigarettes: "Warning: The Surgeon General Has Determined That Cigarette Smoking *Is* Dangerous to Your Health." It clearly does not say *"May* be dangerous to your health."
If you don't smoke we're not about to persuade you to start.	To convince you of what decent, humane, sincere people they are. They don't say anything about how ads such as this have persuaded millions to start smoking in the first place: you ... and perhaps your children.

Another box is headed, "Why do you smoke?"

Ad Copy	Unmasking
With what you've been hearing about smoking these days, you probably	Stop wondering—you might find out the truth: that you've been hypnotized by this kind of campaign. You

Ad Copy	Unmasking
wonder sometimes why you smoke at all.	smoke in large measure because you are an addict—addicted to cigarettes.
Yet you enjoy it.	By now you've come to believe it is the cigarette itself which you enjoy rather than what you are doing while you are smoking it. So let us continue to hypnotize you: look into my eyes and repeat, "I enjoy it."
Because smoking a cigarette can be one of those rare pleasurable private moments. And the chances are you don't want to give up any of that.	The big push begins. First the association of cigarettes with pleasure, a rare and private kind of pleasure. And then a bit of their fancy (il)logic: don't give up "that," implying that if you give up Vantage you will give up your rare and pleasurable moments.
But it is probably the lowest one (i.e., lowest tar cigarette) that will give you enjoyment.	What?! Just enough tar going to your lungs to give you "enjoyment"? This is a coverup. It really means that they've left enough tar to keep you addicted and coming back for more.
And that's why you smoke, right?	Wrong! That is not why you smoke at all. The true answer to why you smoke is that at one time or another

Ad Copy	Unmasking
	you or the person whom you imitated, or the people you were with when you started to smoke, were influenced by advertising such as this, were brainwashed, to put it simply, and now you are hooked, physiologically and psychologically.

A box is headed, "To the 56,000,000 people who smoke cigarettes." (This is supposed to make you feel as if you're in good company.)

Ad Copy	Unmasking
A lot of people have been telling you not to smoke, especially cigarettes with high "tar" and nicotine. But smoking provides you with a pleasure you don't want to give up. Naturally we're prejudiced.	There are more sneaky messages here than you can shake a stick at. Read the copy slowly, carefully paying attention to the particular words and to the overall "tone" of the writing. Do the following exercise *now:* unmask all the components of "the big lie" that you can find in this excerpt. What is left?

Ads such as this support and strengthen your smoking habit each time you read them. In effect, your unconscious is being controlled and you don't know it! Carefully analyzing ads protects you from being influenced by them in this way, keeps you reminded of how diabolical their manipulations are, and illuminates the lies that are being told you in every sentence.

Preliminaries to Changing

This is the preparatory week during which you will lay the groundwork for the changes that will follow. As such it is an extremely important week for you even though you will not be reducing the amount of cigarettes you smoke until next week. It is crucial to build the best foundation that you can by spending some time each day reflecting on what you've read, considering its ramifications, rereading the chapter in whole or in part, and, of course, by doing the exercises diligently.

There are a few things which bear remembering before you get involved in the exercises:

1. All work is an effort against some inertia, therefore it requires the expenditure of energy. You must fully expect to have some difficulties along the way, some resistances or hard spots. Don't be surprised when you meet them. Usually I will have described some procedure to deal with them. Use it, or invent your own procedure if you can think of a better, more powerful one.

2. All change takes time and practice. Be patient with yourself (your SELF), kind to your Self, considerate to your Self as your Self is at work. Don't punish your Self for mistakes; they are inevitable. Forgive your Self and learn from your mistakes so that you can avoid them in the future.

3. There are many ways of becoming a nonsmoker: all at

once, gradually, the first time you try, after repeated attempts, etc. The sooner you become one, obviously, the better off you are; therefore . . . , make *this* the time you quit.

Pitfalls

The major pitfall at this stage of the program is that you will begin rationalizing immediately, somewhat as follows: Well, *I* really don't have to do this particular exercise because: (1) he's only using it as an example—he doesn't really expect me to do it; (2) this doesn't apply to me because my situation is different; (3) I don't have to do it the way he says, I'll just do it my own way. (Most often a way that won't work as well or will work toward the wrong goals.)

Therefore, do *all* exercise assignments in this and the following chapters as precisely and as faithfully as possible.

Exercises

1. Each and every day for one week spend *at least two* (but the more the better) 5-minute periods as follows: get to a quiet spot alone, sit down, close your eyes, take a few long, deep breaths, and then picture yourself throwing away your last package of cigarettes into a blazing fire. As you imagine yourself doing this, take another long, deep breath and relax. If you are not able to get a clear image at first—many people have some difficulty initially—keep practicing: it will get better eventually. It may even take a week or more to perfect. Bring this image to your mind several times during each 5-minute meditation period. Keep a reminder with you to

practice it each day. Do it as precisely as I've described it: breathing and imagining.

2. Once each day look at a different ad for cigarettes and "unmask" it for its sneaky, hypnotic message(s), as was done earlier with the ad for (Disad)-Vantage.

In a recent Facts ad, for example, the serious-looking, middle-aged model looking you square in the eyes is telling you, "I'm realistic. I only smoke Facts." (On a local billboard this was altered to read, "I'm real sick. I only smoke Facts.") And the text says: "We don't want your taste buds to go to sleep." So: "We have smoke scrubbers in our filter." Smoking *does* knock out your sense of taste (and smell), true. But how is it possible to keep your taste buds alive when the rest of you is being slowly killed by the smoking habit . . . and why bother? A dead person with perfectly intact taste buds . . . It makes no sense at all. "Realistic"? Bizarre is more like it!

In the next chapter you will be given additional help and further examples of how to do this simple counterhypnosis. Knowledge is freedom, and you are getting free, free of the control of people whose only interest is in making money at the expense of your health.

3. Each day before you start out (or just before retiring on the night before), mark an "X" with a pen on one cigarette in the pack (no matter whether the pack is new or partially used), in a way that is conspicuous so that you will not miss seeing it. Put this cigarette back in random order so that you don't know its position in the pack. If you smoke more than one pack a day, do this with one cigarette in each pack as soon as you open it.

Smoke as many cigarettes as you like this week; don't try to stop prematurely. But examine each cigarette before you light it. If it is the one with the "X" on it, crumple it up and throw it away. After each "X" cigarette, wait at least one hour before you smoke another cigarette: a form of Russian Roulette for people who want to increase their chances of living, not dying!

4. Examine your rationalizations about stopping smoking, if and when they begin to crop up in your thoughts during the week, and analyze them to uncover their faulty premises. Compare them with the examples given in this chapter. It will help if you *write them down.*

5. Weigh yourself daily and record it. Down the left-hand margin of a piece of paper consecutively list the dates of the next 30 days or so, one date per line. Each day after you weigh yourself, record your weight next to the date.

6. Gradually increase the amount of exercise you do each day. It will be most practical if you pick one form of exercise to emphasize. It can be anything from jumping rope to jogging to walking more vigorously and/or for greater distances than usual. Walk up some stairs that you used to avoid by taking the elevator; leave the bus or park the car a little farther from your destination than you usually would; go for a walk during your lunch hour and window shop or look at the landscape. I am suggesting that you can increase your exercise level in ways that are readily available, pleasant, and easy. Do *not* tire yourself out by doing too much exercise too soon. The increase in exercise should be controlled so that it is not very unpleasant. If it is not a comfortable increase for you, it may be a sign that you are taking on a bit more than you should. Slow down. You'll get there; just keep moving forward at a comfortable pace, and do it regularly—on a *daily* basis. Begin to develop a new habit: an addiction to health. Turn *now* to Chapter 3 and read the section on "Physical Exercise" (p. 87). Do not read anything else in that chapter at this time.

7. Keep a *written* tally of the number of cigarettes you smoke each day this week by putting a mark on a piece of

paper as you smoke each cigarette. You will need to use the average of this week's daily cigarette consumption as a baseline against which to demonstrate your progress, and also to compute just how many cigarettes to cut down by in future weeks. There is evidence, incidentally, that in merely keeping a record of a habit's occurrence you are already beginning to reduce the intensity and frequency of that habit; you may discover yourself smoking less before you expected to.

8. Reread the "Pitfalls" section once each day.

9. Reread this entire "Exercises" section once each day.

Most people who start programs such as this one feel very impatient and want to stop smoking at once. If you begin to feel this way, hang on. Try not to stop until you reach "quitting day." It is only weeks away. What a relief it will be then!

Wait a full week before you begin the next chapter and . . .

> PRACTICE WHAT YOU'VE LEARNED.
> SLOW OR NO PROGRESS WITHOUT IT.

2

⁍

Sophomore

This week you will be making the first major cutback in the number of cigarettes you smoke. During the course of the week, as you work through the material presented in this chapter, you may begin to become aware of certain subtle changes in the way you experience cigarette smoking. Perhaps the smell of someone else's cigarette will suddenly seem annoyingly foul, or the cigarette you were looking forward to won't give you the pleasure you anticipated it would, or an ad you read will reveal itself to be blatantly absurd—or even anger you. There's no telling how or where you will first notice any of these early signals because the shift away from smoking will generally be a gradual one. In any case, stay alert, read carefully, follow the directions explicitly.

The First Cutback

Last week you kept count of the number of cigarettes you smoked each day. Now add up these daily figures and divide the total by seven (days) in order to get a daily average. Divide this figure by three (one-third). Subtract this number from your daily average. The remainder is the number of cigarettes you will smoke each day this week: one-third fewer cigarettes each day than you did last week. In other words, each day of this week you will smoke only two-thirds as many cigarettes as you smoked on the average of each day of last week. There will be another cutback next week and another one the week following that. About two weeks from now you will not be smoking at all.

Since most people do not find this first slight reduction to be very difficult, I have described many of the new procedures for dealing with and accomplishing these cutbacks in the following two or three chapters, where the going may become a bit more demanding.

By all means, if you discover during the course of this week that you are among those who need more help in accomplishing this first cutback, turn to the next chapter, Chapter 3, and read the section entitled "The Allies." Read *only* that section in advance, and only if you really need to; otherwise stay with the sequence of one chapter per week.

The "allies" are procedures that have been designed either:

1. to maximize your power over the smoking habit.
2. to minimize the power of the habit itself.
3. to make you more comfortable as you go about quitting.

The Health Bank

For each cigarette that you eliminate you are to save a certain sum of money in a separate place—as much as you can afford without taxing your budget too severely, but *at least* as much as the cigarettes themselves cost you: a Health Bank of sorts. By the time the program is over, three or four weeks from now, you will have a sum of money which you will be able to use for whatever you choose. This is not an optional feature of the program, so be *sure* you make use of it. The money you save can add up to quite a tidy sum in just a short time—money to use to reward yourself for work well done.

Long after the program is over and you have stopped smoking you may decide to continue saving the money formerly spent on cigarettes and use it for more creative and enjoyable purposes. For instance, you might want to spend it directly on yourself, buying either an object or an experience that you've wanted, or you might want to donate it to a charitable organization which supports work in conquering cancer, emphysema, or heart disease, and in educating the public to the dangers of smoking (e.g., the American Heart Association or the American Lung Association or the American Cancer Society).[1] You may decide to use the money as a contribution to an organization devoted exclusively to anti-smoking efforts, a group which is less well known and must operate on a tiny budget, such as GASP (Group Against Smoking Pollution), for instance, which actively crusades against smoking where it interferes with the rights of nonsmokers, or ASH (Action on Smoking and Health). If you smoke one pack of cigarettes a day you are spending about $200 a year—money going up in smoke.

1. Address of ACS: 777 Third Ave., N.Y., N.Y. 10017
Address of AHA: 7320 Greenville Ave., Dallas, Texas 75231
Address of ALA: 1740 Broadway, N.Y., N.Y. 10019
Address of GASP: P.O. Box 4400, San Francisco, Calif. 94101
Address of ASH: 2000 H St. N.W., Washington, D.C. 20006

Selecting an "Anticigarette"

Cutting down on the brand of cigarettes that you have been used to smoking is likely to be more difficult than cutting down on a brand that you are unfamiliar with, especially if it is a brand that you *dislike.*

Therefore, take the time *now* to select an "anticigarette," a cigarette that in many ways reverses the major characteristics of the cigarette you presently smoke. (The reverse of "cigaret" nearly spells "tragic.") In other words, select a brand that you are *least* likely to enjoy. If you smoke filters, select a nonfilter; if you smoke nonfilters, select a filter; if you smoke menthol, select a nonmenthol; if you smoke a high tar cigarette, select a "low tar" cigarette; if you smoke a "low tar" cigarette, select a cigarette high in tars; if you smoke regular size, select king or queen size, etc.

The idea is to select a cigarette, if possible, that you despise. I say "if possible" because it has been my experience that smokers who despise certain brands of cigarettes are surprised at how quickly they can get used to them, and even begin to like them. Smokers, like other addicts, are remarkably adaptable—just so long as they can get their "fix."

The Self versus the Robot Smoker

People tend to refer to the cigarettes they usually smoke as "my" brand. How did you come to select the brand of cigarettes you smoke? What influenced your choice?

· Was it the brand your father smoked, or your mother, or a friend or lover, or someone whom you admired or felt close to, or wanted to be like?

• Is it a brand you finally arrived at after trying a number of others? If so, why did you change brands? Was it for "taste,"[2] tar and nicotine content, looks and packaging image?

• Do you have certain associations with the brand you smoke that you don't have with others? What are these associations based upon? Search your memory.

Think of the ads for the particular cigarette that you smoke. What do they emphasize? What kinds of people appear in them? What kinds of images do they use? What kind of messages do the ads convey?

Consider these questions carefully. They are meant to be answered. Answer them before you read further.

No matter what reason you give yourself as to why you smoke the particular brand you do, it is likely to be a rationalization of one sort or another. You have been more influenced by advertising than you realize.

Most people don't want to admit either to themselves or to others that they have been influenced in this way; they are defensive about it, try to cover it up, try to deny it. They don't want to admit that they were duped—it is an embarrassment to them.

Each one of you likes to believe that you are too clever or clear thinking to have had the wool pulled over your eyes. Yet, of course, there is simply no other way to explain how it happens that there are over 50 million smokers in the United States alone. Mass hypnosis is the only possible explanation.

You have been hypnotized. There are no two ways about it.

"Your" brand of cigarettes is actually not "your"brand at

---

2. Studies have shown that when people are blindfolded they are not able reliably to discern the difference in taste between one cigarette and another—even between filters and nonfilters.

all. The "you" or the Self, the most basic, most essential part of who you are, is always and forever a *nonsmoker*. You must have been carefully taught or brainwashed into starting and continuing to smoke.

For most of you this brainwashing first occurred during your adolescence, a time when you were more vulnerable, more susceptible to influence through peer pressure, than at any other time in your life.

Smoking does not come easily or naturally to us; the pressure to do so must be very great and very persistent. In adolescence the pressure to conform, to be "sophisticated" or "debonair," to look like a grownup is "supposed" to look, to be one of the crowd instead of a "weirdo" or a "square" or some other form of nonconformist, is relentless. The consequence of not conforming is too often loneliness and ostracism—a great and painful price to pay for being your Self.

For those of you who started to smoke later in life, the reasons are usually very similar:

1. You experienced some sort of stress and smoking distracted you from it.

2. You had a desire, either conscious or unconscious, to identify with a certain image that you associated with smoking.

So you bent your will—usually with a lot of encouragement—and before long you were a smoker: hooked, addicted, a cigarette junkie. As you lost control and became more dominated by this addiction, you began to smoke in an increasingly automatic fashion. Half the time you were not even aware that you were smoking. The habit got away from you. Eventually you behaved as though controlled by some force or power outside yourself, very much as a robot does: an automaton. In fact, a kind of smoking robot is just what part of you becomes once you're hooked. I've called this addicted part the *Robot Smoker* (or R.S.) throughout the book.

But the healthy Self continues to exist within each of you, weakened perhaps but ready to be revived, brought back to power, ready to take charge again and restore health and reason.

Given the proper support and encouragement, the life-affirming principle within each of us, which I have called the Self in this book, can defeat the destructive, life-denying Robot Smoker, the R.S.

This is the major operating principle of this program, and this is what you must make happen: you must increase your human capacity to choose freedom over the bondage of addiction, health over disease, the Self over the Robot Smoker, life over death.

The Role of Hypnosis

What the cigarette manufacturers imply through their nauseatingly ubiquitous ads (showing "beautiful" people enjoying the marvels of the great outdoors, or serenely relaxing, or having a romantic moment or a lighthearted, humorous one, all accompanied by a cigarette) is that these healthy pleasures will be diminished without that cigarette, that smoking a cigarette logically enhances these pleasures.

They know that if you can be or have been brainwashed into believing this you certainly will not want to give up smoking because you don't want to do without the accompanying pleasures or their enhancement. Sounds like double-talk, doesn't it?

This form of double-talk is, of course, sheer hypnosis in its most orthodox sense and nothing less, and whether you are aware of it or not, you are or have been the victim of this hypnosis. But this is not the only form of hypnotism going on. Self-hypnotism takes up where ad-hypnotism leaves off.

After one has smoked for many years, the habit pattern inevitably becomes linked to certain frequently occurring life events, many of them pleasurable in themselves. Some of the more common linkages are:

- Smoking with coffee.
- Smoking after a meal.
- Smoking while going for a walk.
- Smoking while watching T.V.
- Smoking before going to bed.
- Smoking upon waking from sleep.
- Smoking while sitting at the desk.
- Smoking while talking on the phone.
- Smoking while having a drink.
- Smoking while engaging in conversation.
- Smoking while reading.
- Smoking while driving a car.
- Smoking when someone else lights up.
- Smoking after sex.

This list is by no means complete: consider other linkages, many of which were originally taught you by the ads or by social conventions which have been exploited by ads. In this respect, as a smoker you are behaving like a conditioned animal in a laboratory, very much like Pavlov's dog who came to salivate every time a bell was rung, because the dog was originally taught that the bell was a signal that food would soon follow; a bell–food linkage was established. Yet the bell wasn't what the dog was salivating about, the food was. Certain situations are pleasurable in themselves, and after they become linked to smoking a cigarette, the cigarette, like the bell, becomes the signal for the pleasure. Soon you begin to respond to the cigarette as if *it* were the pleasure. Each time you participate in one of these linked situations you begin to experience the desire for a cigarette. This is an automatic and unconscious process, called a conditioned reflex. And each time you repeat it, it becomes stronger, more likely to be further repeated, further strengthened. A vicious cycle gets set up.

As you examine cigarette ads you can begin to see how you have come to form some of your particular associations to smoking. They did not occur accidentally; they are a fundamental part of the advertising schemes used by the tobacco companies.

Obviously, many of the linkages in your smoking habit were not taught to you directly by ads; some were modeled upon your own personal observations of how others use cigarettes: relatives, friends, strangers, even movie stars. Still other linkages may even have been of your own design. But it is undeniably true that there is an important back-and-forth interplay between these other models and the ads. Who did the models pattern themselves after originally? Where did it all begin?

At least two processes are going on simultaneously: the ads mimic and exploit patterns that already exist among habitual smokers, and at the same time they attempt to create new associations that will expand the practice of the habit among the general population. They've even begun to infiltrate and co-opt sporting events once again (at one time many professional athletes posed for cigarette commercials). Virginia Slims sponsors tennis tournaments, and ads showing people lighting up after they've finished exercising are becoming commonplace; they suggest, among other things, that you follow up your healthy activity, exercise, with an unhealthy one, smoking. Where will this insanity end?

Another thing you should consider: the more of these associations or linkages you have and the more often they occur (the more conditioned reflexes you have to smoking), the more cigarettes you smoke—and the happier the cigarette manufacturers are! And remember, the usefulness of an idea to a cigarette manufacturer is a direct measure of its use*less*ness to you!

Stop reading for a few minutes *now* and *write* down a list of your personal linkages or conditioned reflex areas. In which situations do you almost always smoke or want to smoke? Select any one of these areas for the first project of this week's phase of the program. It will be the one situation where you will deliberately refrain from smoking. More about this later, in the "Exercises" section.

The Myth of Symptom Substitution

A major myth has grown up around stopping smoking that needs to be explored and exploded before we go any further. Based upon an assumption known as "symptom substitution," there is, unfortunately, a commonly held belief that when a person gives up a habit such as cigarette smoking a new bad habit *always and automatically* "pops up" and takes its place.

Believing in this idea, of course, is a good way to *make* it come true, just as worrying about having a car accident may make you so nervous that you actually have one which you would have avoided had you not been so tensely anticipating it. And sometimes the part of you that doesn't want to stop smoking actually may cause you to *want* to hold on to an idea such as "symptom substitution."

Don't let yourself fall for this kind of overly pat thinking. There is no scientifically valid reason for the notion that giving up a negative habit automatically leads to acquiring another bad habit. In many, if not most, instances the reverse proves to be true. Numerous studies have shown that giving up a destructive habit is often accompanied by feelings of greater general well-being and greater self-confidence. These in turn can encourage you to work on eliminating other destructive habits. Many people have told me that their lives started to change radically for the better when they quit smoking.

As you become a nonsmoker, therefore, contrary to what you may have feared, eventually you are likely to find yourself sleeping better, feeling less irritable during the day, more relaxed, and having no more trouble maintaining your normal weight than you ever did. These changes take time, but after a short while you will almost definitely feel more energetic and awake, since you will be increasing your daily intake of oxygen as you reduce your intake of the poisonous gases found in cigarette smoke. Be on the lookout for these and other positive changes; you will probably begin to notice them in small, subtle ways within a few weeks or less.

You don't *necessarily* have to suffer if you give up cigarettes; many people don't. You may be lucky enough to be among those who don't experience some temporary discomfort or disturbance in various bodily functions, but there is also a good likelihood that you will be discomfited to some degree: each one of us is different in this regard. After all, your body needs time to adjust to doing without all the poisons in cigarette smoke—a withdrawal effect such as occurs in all drug addictions. This is known in the parlance of drug treatment as "detoxification."

If you have heard stories of pain and suffering from people you know who stopped smoking (and who of us has not heard them?), or if you have made previous attempts to give up smoking and have experienced these miseries yourself, you will be glad to know that this program will devote a good deal of attention to alleviating or constructively dealing with them. Many of the exercises in the following chapters have been designed with this interest specifically in mind. In fact, *the more diligently you follow the program, the more likely you will be to prevent many of the more common difficulties from arising in the first place.* Remember, too, it just may be that your situation will be closer to that of the countless ex-smokers who found stopping *less* difficult than originally anticipated.

It bears repeating that the idea that you will *automatically* gain weight or become temporarily insomniac or have some other negative habit "pop out" if you quit smoking just doesn't hold water. This false notion is often popularized by people who are rationalizing their own smoking habits (people who say, "I'm only smoking so as not to gain weight," or "It helps me to keep awake and alert."). In the event that you should experience an increase in any other troublesome behavior pattern while you are cutting down on or after you stop smoking, it can and should be dealt with separately.

Consider that any such pattern was there all the time but hidden by a smoke screen, camouflaged by your smoking habit. These other patterns are *not* likely to be freshly developed destructive replacements for smoking but just the next habit-links in what may be a chain, usually a small chain, of troublesome behaviors. In the next chapters you will learn ways of analyzing and dealing with these trouble spots.

Do you have such a chain? What are its habit-links? Don't forget, no matter what the next link is in the chain, *if* there *is* another link, there is practically no chance that it is anywhere as harmful as cigarette smoking, though in some cases it may be temporarily more annoying. No matter what it is, something can be done about it—and what is done about it won't have anything to do with smoking.

Undermining the Robot Smoker

In order to break the smoking habit—indeed, in order to break *any* habit—you must "relocate" the source of its control from the unconscious to the conscious mind (this is fundamentally what is meant by the rather overworked term "consciousness raising"). You will need to raise your level of awareness about the way your "knee jerks," or automatic responses, operate. In effect, ultimately you must banish the Robot Smoker from its comfortable home within you. *This is a gradual process.* Therefore, from now on each time you reach for a cigarette your healthy Self will be putting the addicted part, or Robot Smoker, through a little ritual, one which will require a slight, conscious effort.

Wrap your cigarettes. By wrapping the pack of cigarettes in a piece of newspaper held on by a rubber band in such a way that a cigarette cannot be removed without taking off the band and unwrapping the paper, you will be raising your awareness and beginning to "de-robotize" yourself. This is the next step in gaining ownership of your Self (as in, "I just haven't been myself lately," or, "I feel as if I'm getting back to myself again.").

If you are asked by anyone why you have your cigarettes wrapped, say something like, "It's part of a program I'm engaged in to stop smoking." Always remember to stay with the spirit of this program, which is to "go public" whenever it seems reasonable to do so. If people ask about the program, they deserve an honest answer; give them one.

You will need all the help you can get in order to accomplish the goal of taking your habit away from the control of the R.S. and bringing it into the control of the Self. There is real benefit to be had from demonstrating to your

Self that you can, *rather easily* and *immediately,* exercise some control over the smoking habit by wrapping the pack in the manner described. It can help to boost your self-confidence, and incidentally, as I mentioned before, getting control of an injurious habit frequently leads to quite an *overall* improvement in self-confidence. You may eventually begin to feel like tackling other unfinished business in your life once you have kicked the smoking habit. You may consider other habit patterns to improve: increasing the amount of exercise you do, for example, or cutting down on the amount of junk food or sweets that you consume. But a word of warning: do not begin too many Self-improvement programs at once. It is wisest to pace yourself and focus your energy on one or two areas (at most) at a time. Taking on too much at once is a good way to exhaust your Self into failure.

You are actively going to strengthen your Self control by the use of *delay periods.* From this week on, between the time you become aware of wanting to smoke a cigarette and the time you actually take the cigarette from the pack, you are to wait 5 minutes. Although at first this may seem to be a long time, after smoking a few cigarettes this way you will probably hardly notice the minutes passing.

In addition to this *pre*-cigarette delay period you will use a delay period occasionally *while* you are smoking. In this case you are to delay by counting slowly from one through five (about 5 seconds) before taking the drag you were about to take. Do this at random, whenever you think of it, at least two or three times with each cigarette you smoke.

Inevitably, you will notice that from time to time you have become distracted during the 5-minute delay period and you have altogether forgotten the cigarette. This is a bonus—you may actually end up smoking fewer cigarettes this week than the amount you planned on cutting down to! What does this say about what you may have thought was your ironclad compulsion to smoke? And what does it 	[illegible] about what you may have come to think was the strength 	[illegible] your smoking habit, the number of cigarettes you "needed" to get through the day?

Perhaps you have even been hypnotizing yourself in these areas, convincing yourself about something that wasn't true, was never really tested. Have you done this? What have you told yourself about your smoking habit? What are your personal myths about smoking? When was the last time you examined them? These questions are meant to be taken seriously; do not read on any further until you have actually reflected on them and answered them. Don't take anything for granted that you may have told yourself about your smoking habits or your "need": the cigarette-smoking habit rests upon ideas that have usually been unexamined, notions that are actually quite different from the way they appear to be on the surface. Ultimately it rests on pure nonsense, on a fabric of untruths, whether you're hearing it from Madison Avenue or the Robot Smoker, as you will gradually realize when you get deeper into the program.

The use of delay periods is particularly helpful in taking the habit away from the control of the addicted part of ourselves (the Robot Smoker) and bringing it into the control of the healthy part (the Self). Your acts of smoking will gradually become deautomatized. It isn't always an easy process, this transformation of the smoking habit, and it is almost never effortless. The Robot Smoker is likely to protest about one thing or another in order to dissuade you from progressing on your course. The Robot Smoker is a voice within you, the voice of a saboteur telling you anything that will keep you a smoker.

Perhaps even now the R.S. is telling you something about how much "trouble" stopping smoking is—all these techniques, so much to do, etc., etc. Don't fall for this jive; it is a

disguised sales pitch. Like other rationalizations about smoking, it needs to be unmasked and robbed of its power to
influence you as soon as it arises. The amount of "trouble" it
is to stop smoking is ultimately insignificant when compared
with the amount of trouble it is to smoke, trouble in every
way you can think of: trouble to remember to buy cigarettes
and to buy enough so you won't run out, to make sure you
have matches on hand or have filled your cigarette lighter;
trouble with the cough you get occasionally or often; trouble
with the smoke stinging your eyes at times, with the brown
stains left on fingers or teeth, with the stale smell of cigarettes
around you; trouble wondering if they allow smoking where
you are going, or if someone will object to your smoking;
trouble caused by worries such as burning holes in your
clothing, or falling asleep while smoking and burning more
than just your clothing, or teaching your child how to be a
smoker (children whose parents *don't* smoke eventually
become smokers themselves substantially *less* often than
children who have one parent who smokes; children who are
unlucky enough to have both parents smoke, of course, are
most likely to become smokers themselves). And, of course,
you are constantly troubled, consciously or unconsciously,
that you are damaging your health.

Remind yourself of these facts as you are putting each
aspect of this program into action. Once again, if you look at
the subject clearly and honestly, there is not a single valid
reason for remaining a smoker, not one! Whatever discipline
it takes to stop is more than worth it.

Unmasking Ads: The Names

Now let's look at some other aspects of those ads for
cigarettes that bombard our consciousnesses everywhere we
turn.

Have you ever thought about the names used for cigarettes? Just like the rest of the copy in the ad, they've been psychologically designed to brainwash you into having positive associations about smoking. The ad agencies of Madison Avenue are telling you to smoke Now (and get cancer later), Merit (De-Merit), Vantage (Disad-Vantage), True (False), Kool (Hot), More (Less), Real (Fake), and the like. The names of some cigarettes cluster around associations of royalty and aristocracy (Kent, Montclair, Viceroy, Regency, Carlton, Parliament, Raleigh, Marlboro, Tareyton, Winston, Chesterfield), in order, I suppose, to make you feel more dignified and "respectable" when you light up. The names of others seem to be playing to economic worries, concerns about inflation and the like (Max and More: maximum harm and more disease). Have you noticed that since the country has come into economically hard times the cigarette companies have been pushing the trend to longer and longer cigarettes in order to appeal to your otherwise reasonable desire to get more for your money? (Get more emphysema for your money with our cigarettes!).

They've even exploited the women's movement by designing cigarettes to appeal specifically to the female sex with Virginia Slims, Eve, and Dawn. The copy on some of these ads infers that if a woman wants to be "with it" she ought to smoke a "modern woman's cigarette." All that talk about "You've come a long way, baby" is supposed to make you feel liberated and independent if you smoke the brand being touted.

Any woman who is influenced by this slick and malicious nonsense has a long way to go to be liberated—she's in the process of becoming a slave to a new master. Lung cancer rates among women have risen alarmingly since women have been smoking more cigarettes, and they have been smoking more since specific ad campaigns have been directed at them.

Among the most viciously cynical approaches to be

exploited in the serious and potentially lethal matter of selling cigarettes to the public has been the use of humor as the principal sales pitch (e.g., Long Johns, Benson & Hedges). They've even managed to buy Charlie Chaplin! His image of the lovable tramp, which has such warm, positive associations for most who have seen his films, appeared on Tramps. You can bet that people who smoked Tramps and developed shortness of breath or a nagging cough aren't feeling very warm and loving about Charlie Chaplin. (Tramps has since been withdrawn from the market because of poor sales.)

When Evan, my nine-year-old son, heard that I was writing a section about the naming of cigarettes he said, "They should name a cigarette God. It would sell by the millions." And he's right. Think of the advertising possibilities: "Tense? Overworked? Lonely? Bring God into your life and relax. Remember, God is peace (here a picture of a man or woman smoking while looking blissfully relaxed, a church or synagogue in the background), and God is love." (Closeup of a couple facing one another, looking into each other's eyes, each with a cigarette in their mouth, he lighting hers, she lighting his, and the warm glow of their matches illuminating their deep, intense, yet tender gaze.)

The cigarette manufacturers are coming out with new cigarettes faster than I can keep track of them. As I was writing this book, about five new cigarettes were introduced on the market, and even as I wrote this section I discovered a full page ad in my morning paper for yet another one: Eagles. Why Eagles? Perhaps, the eagle being the national bird, to capitalize on the recent bicentennial. But its major advertising gimmick is to play on your desire to economize in these hard times. The text reads in bold type: "New Eagle 20's. Now you can save a nickel on every pack of cigarettes you smoke."

Why just think, if you smoke as many as three packs a day you will have saved 15 cents a day, $1.05 per week, $31.50 a month, $378.00 a year! But ... one day in the hospital costs well over $200.00 in most instances, and a missed day of work costs how much? The treatment for cancer costs thousands. A missed day, or week, or month, or year, or five years—or twenty years, because you died sooner than you would have from natural causes—is beyond cost.

When I was a boy, about twenty-five or thirty years ago, I can recall there being only about six or seven brands of cigarettes sold at the local store. Now they come in several sizes and colors, with various filters, in different containers. I recently saw an article in which 145 varieties were listed! [3] An acquaintance pointed out that this wild proliferation of cigarette varieties is in some measure a by-product of the government's decision to ban cigarette advertising from the airwaves (radio and T.V.)—as of January 2, 1971. The cigarette manufacturers, fearing that the ban would cause sales to drop, increased the kinds of cigarettes in order to compensate for the reduction in media coverage (and, of course, increased their advertising in the printed media where no ban exists: newspapers, magazines, billboards). Since 1971 over 105 new varieties of cigarettes have been marketed.[4]

The printed media are becoming more and more saturated with cigarette advertising, penetrating every segment of the population; and as advertising techniques become more psychologically sophisticated (and therefore more powerfully hypnotic-inductive-manipulative), the media can be directed to zero-in on a particular facet of the population. This way of focusing makes advertising far more potent—like a concen-

3. *Chicago Daily News,* April 22, 1976, p. 16.
4. *Business Week,* December 6, 1976, p. 64.

trated ray from an X-ray machine. The closer an ad can aim at your particular personal characteristics (your age, sex, dress, skin color, tastes, concerns, life style, values), the more likely it is to influence you. More and more particularizing of this kind is being done in ads, and since there are so many different kinds of people, this becomes another reason for the stupendous growth of cigarette varieties. There are enormous numbers of people still smoking (about 55 million adults in the United States smoke) despite all we now know about cigarettes causing disease and death.

At this rate, if there is no change in public policy, in twenty years there may be a thousand varieties of cigarettes, their numbers increasing as fast as the cancers they create. At the very least, aside from banning cigarette smoking in public places, the government should curtail the expansion of cigarette varieties. It would make much more sense to do this than merely to require the feeble warning on cigarette ads and packages—"Warning: The Surgeon General Has Determined That Cigarette Smoking Is Dangerous to Your Health"—set off in small print in a little box; this totally ineffectual warning has probably not been of much help to anyone in stopping smoking.

It is a myth that people are smoking more because the times are more stressful. They are smoking more because the tobacco interests are hell-bent on making money and haven't a care for sane and reasonable human values. They aren't concerned with the harm they promote so long as the revenues keep coming in.

Where the name of the cigarette isn't playing games with your thoughts or feelings, you may *always* be certain that some other component of the ad is manipulating you in some other way. Keep reading those ads and unmasking them until you are doing it automatically. Unmasking is your best defense against brainwashing. Later I will analyze some of the visual images used in the cigarette ads and show what they are trying to get you to believe and how they work to influence you without your being aware of it.

Pitfalls

Read the "Pitfalls" section at the end of Chapter 1 once more. Now add: "All these things I need to do in order to stop smoking . . . it's a lot of trouble—it takes so much time, so much thought, so much effort—I wonder if it's worth the bother after all."

Exercises

1. Continue to visualize *at least once a day,* for about 5 minutes, the image of throwing your last package of cigarettes into a fire (as described in the first exercise of Chapter 1).

2. Continue to unmask cigarette ads each day, paying attention especially to the text of the ad and the names of the cigarettes.

3. Calculate the average number of cigarettes you smoked per day last week, and *as you begin each day this week,* take with you exactly two-thirds of that average and no more. If you buy a new pack during the course of the day, put aside all cigarettes that exceed that number as soon as you open the pack. Smoke only two-thirds (or a little less) of your average each day.

4. At the beginning of each day, wrap your pack of cigarettes or cigarette case in a sheet of newspaper and hold

it on with a rubber band so that in order to take a cigarette you must remove the rubber band before unwrapping the paper. Replace the band and the paper after *each* cigarette.

5. Save a certain amount of money in a "Health Bank" for each cigarette less than the average number you smoked each day last week—as much as you can *comfortably* afford.

6. Slightly increase the amount of exercise you do this week so that it is a bit more than you did last week. Don't bite off more than you can chew: the increase should be definite but gradual, not exhausting.

7. Change to an "anticigarette"—a brand that is least likely to be enjoyed by the Robot Smoker.

8. Delay about 5 minutes between the time you get a desire for each cigarette and the time you actually light it. Also, on occasion (about two or three times for each cigarette), count slowly from one through five before you take the next drag.

9. Don't smoke in one habit area (while you are on the phone, after meals, etc.). Discontinue the particular activity if you decide to smoke. Disconnect those linkages to smoking.

10. Continue to examine your rationalizations.

11. Weigh yourself daily and record it on your weight chart.

12. Reread the "Pitfalls" and the "Exercises" sections of this chapter once each day. This is most important.

Wait a full week before you begin the next chapter, and . . .

PRACTICE WHAT YOU'VE LEARNED.
SLOW OR NO PROGRESS WITHOUT IT.

3

Junior

Aside from describing what an addictive habit is and how and why it works, this chapter will introduce you to a little-discussed but enormously important concept: autonomic conditioning. It is one of the most basic—if not *the* most basic—factors underlying the smoking habit. You'll be making the second cutback on your cigarette consumption this week, so lots of good help will be provided for your Self in its war with the Robot Smoker—ease for the difficulties you may encounter as you break the habit's grip on you.

Smoking: Bad Habit or Addiction?

Technically speaking, behavioral habits which involve the regular use of a drug are called *addictions* when two major characteristics are present:

1. In the early stages especially, the person using the drug requires greater and greater amounts of it in order to produce the desired effects—tolerance for the drug increases substantially from its initial level.

2. When the drug is reduced or terminated, withdrawal effects such cramps, vomiting, tremors, increase in or loss of

appetite, irritability, chills, or insomnia may occur, and the addict experiences a craving for the drug as a way of reducing these withdrawal symptoms.

It is ridiculous to quibble about whether cigarette smoking is an addiction or "merely" a powerful bad habit. It certainly satisfies the definition of an addiction in every important way, and that definition relates only to the chemical component of addictions.

But what about the nonchemical components? It doesn't much matter what you call it, smoking surely hooks you in more ways than just chemically. In all probability you are even hooked to some extent on the magic of striking the match (or flicking a cigarette lighter) and producing a flame—a bit of sparkling life from an inert object—and hooked as well on the sight of exhaling the smoke. (Don't you often exhale it in a pattern: through the nostrils? through the mouth? in smoke rings? all at once? in bursts? half through the mouth and half through the nose?) It is precisely this level of influence, a level of such extraordinary subtlety at times, that makes the smoking habit or addiction so pernicious. It operates on you in ways that you have never even considered.

Try the following experiment two or three times this week. Smoke a *whole* cigarette with your eyes completely closed at the same time that you reduce your sense of smell by breathing in and out exclusively through your mouth. You probably know already that smoking is not going to be as "pleasurable" under these circumstances, and now you can begin to understand why. The act of smoking is connected to far more than just the feeling of smoke filling your lungs and the consequent change in your blood chemistry; *all* your sense organs are "tied" to it! Your eyes become tied to the match-lighting "ceremony," to seeing the smoke coming out of your mouth and nose, to seeing others smoking, to reading cigarette ads; your ears are tied to the sound of the match or lighter striking and to the sound of your inhaling and exhaling; your nose becomes conditioned to the smell of the tobacco and smoke; your tactile (touch) sense gets tied to the feeling of the cigarette in your hand or lips; and your taste buds certainly get tied to the tars and other chemicals in the cigarette smoke.

If cigarette smoking does not exactly fit the medical dictionary's definition of an addiction, it certainly qualifies as a great deal more than just another bad habit. Let's call it an "addictive habit" and be done with it. It's perfectly clear that you're all tied up if you're a smoker: you are less free, as is any prisoner.

A Hidden Destroyer: Autonomic Conditioning

You can be certain that the sensory linkages keeping you connected to your addictive habit—the ones mentioned above—are only one part of the picture, and probably not the most significant part. Another part is going on *inside* you and, of course, is much more difficult to observe. It is a process called "autonomic conditioning," and in this case it is particularly destructive.

Autonomic conditioning refers to a situation in which the functioning of the internal organs of the body such as the heart, digestive tract, liver, glands, etc., which are normally regulated by control centers within the brain, become artificially influenced by an unnatural mechanism, such as the repeated introduction of chemicals into the body, which by-passes these control centers. The other organs as well as the brain itself are affected in this manner and are then repeatedly forced to behave abnormally in one way or another. The functioning of the organs may speed up, slow down, exhibit erratic fluctuations in activity, or become affected in other unusual ways. These abnormal alterations may occur anywhere in the body, affecting, for example, heartbeat rate or tempo, breathing rate, blood pressure, general metabolism, flow of gastric juices, and elimination of wastes.

The healthy body is constantly adjusting itself in order to cope maximally with changing circumstances, and without these adjustments or adaptations we would surely die. By and large most of these life circumstances occur in a fairly random order. For instance, we may temporarily have to speed up for a while *occasionally,* as when we run to catch a bus or play tennis. The heart beats faster as we are getting this physical exercise and as it does so it pumps more oxygen around the body.

This kind of speed-up induced by physical exercise and accompanied by an increase in oxygen supply is healthy and invigorating; it builds the body. After the reason for the temporary speed-up is no longer present (the bus is boarded, the tennis game is over), the body gradually and automatically returns to its normal level of functioning. This balancing process is called "homeostasis." The organs rest and approach their baseline or normal resting rates (basal metabolism). Rest, of course, is restorative and recuperative to all living things. Without it illness and even death eventually result.

Let's look at what happens to these bodily processes when you smoke a cigarette.

The chemicals in the smoke, nicotine as well as others, cause the heart and other organs to work faster and harder while the vital oxygen intake is *decreased,* not increased as it is when you are exercising. This happens because the smoke has a high percentage of carbon monoxide in it, a deadly gas which interferes with the absorption of oxygen by the blood.

In effect, the body is being made to work harder while being deprived of its proper oxygen supply, and as this is going on, neither the useless or harmful by-products of this speeded-up metabolism, nor the chemicals you introduced by inhaling the smoke, are being healthily dispensed as rapidly as they should be (and as they are when you are exercising and sweating, breathing deeply and vigorously).

Obviously, this is a prescription for illness *par excellence:* the body is overworked, under-rested, undernourished, and functioning in a polluted environment!

And here's the clincher, the place where autonomic conditioning occurs. After a while you become comfortable with what really *should* be a highly *un*comfortable state of affairs; you grow used to these artificial levels of functioning. A process called habituation, or adaptation, takes place. Your body either stops sending your brain signals that something is wrong and needs changing, or your brain stops processing these signals. You begin to crave a cigarette even at times when there is no *external* trigger such as another person smoking, or a cup of coffee. You think you are taking that next cigarette just because you're "in the mood" for one, or whatever. But what is actually going on *without your awareness* is that your heart, for instance, has been gradually—homeostatically—returning to its normal baseline rate of about 73 beats per minute from its artificially increased rate of, let's say, 95 beats per minute, a rate provoked by the last cigarette you smoked perhaps 35 minutes ago. When the heartbeat crosses a certain subjective threshold on its way back to normal, let's say, 80 beats per minute, you begin to experience the mild discomfort that is called a "craving" by some, or a "need" by others (as in, "I need a cigarette").

In fact, it does take the heart well over an hour after each cigarette is smoked to return to its normal rate of beating. You then smoke the next cigarette, drive the heartbeat back up and feel "comfortable" again! In this way, until you go to sleep in the evening, you prevent your metabolism from ever reaching its near-basal level and allowing your body to get the rest it should have. Your heart is in a nearly constant state of overexertion.

Of course, an inevitable and destructive side-effect of this is that all the extra work the heart has to do under such conditions tires it out. The blood is being pumped throughout the body at an increased and abnormal rate; the blood pressure is driven up, fatty deposits are laid down on the walls of the blood vessels more rapidly, narrowing them and causing them to lose their elasticity, thereby driving the pressure still higher and taxing the heart further. A vicious cycle has begun and it is being helped along each time you inhale. Now you can understand why smokers have a higher incidence than nonsmokers of heart attacks, atherosclerosis, Reynaud's disease (coldness due to impaired circulation of blood to the extremities of the fingers and toes), strokes, and dozens of other diseases and harmful conditions.

If you think of all these diseases, you will notice that by and large they have one surprising thing in common—they are *diseases of aging!* You guessed it, *smokers grow prematurely old* in nearly every way: inside and outside, heart to skin, for all the reasons I've mentioned; they grow old sooner and die sooner than nonsmokers.

The inescapable message of all this, put as succinctly as I've heard it, is: "The body is not a smoking machine. If you want a smoking machine, get a fireplace."

An Experiment in Autonomic Conditioning

You can see just how thoroughly, from within and without (autonomic conditioning and advertising), the smoker is being controlled by her or his Robot Smoker. If you want to become wholly and comfortably free of the desire to smoke, not merely a temporary nonsmoker holding on for dear life and clenching your teeth as the R.S. beats on you to smoke, you must continue in every possible way to disconnect your Self from the control of the Robot Smoker. You must drive a psychological wedge between them so that your Self can be separate and free enough to combat your addicted part and do its healing work.

Before, I described a technique in which you were to light and smoke a cigarette with your eyes shut in order to demonstrate the way your smoking "enjoyment" is governed by certain external events. To demonstrate the way your smoking governs internal events and they in turn govern your desire for a cigarette is a somewhat more difficult matter, but it can be done if you concentrate.

Perform the following experiment two or three times this week. Sit down facing a blank wall in as quiet a room as you can find, as free as possible from distractions. Wait a full minute or two until your heartbeat seems normal and at rest (obviously, this means that you must not have smoked for at least an hour before you perform this experiment, nor should you have just finished doing vigorous exercise). Then smoke *two* cigarettes, one directly after the other at a somewhat faster rate than usual. Lighting a cigarette and either closing your eyes or staring at the blank wall in front of you, try to focus your attention inside your body.

What effects do you notice on your heartbeat, your pulse (place your index and middle fingers on the inside of the wrist an inch or so above the thumb and press gently in order to feel your pulse), your equilibrium or sense of balance, the feeling in your stomach? Do you notice any visual, auditory (hearing), gustatory (taste), or olfactory (smell) changes that you may not have noticed before or paid attention to? How about the temperature in your fingers and toes? What changes did you notice in any part of your body?

Immediately upon finishing the first cigarette, light up the second; two cigarettes smoked consecutively will further heighten your awareness of what goes on inside you with each single cigarette you smoke. You will be able to notice these changes more clearly by condensing the event called "smoking a cigarette" because usually you dilute these effects by spreading the activity out over a longer time. Of course, many of you who are chain smokers (chained to smoking) have more or less gotten used to smoking two or more cigarettes one after the other and have adapted to the poisons. If you are a chain smoker, therefore, it will be especially important to smoke the two cigarettes quite rapidly so as to produce the condensation effect necessary to this exercise.

Way Back When:
Recalling Your First Cigarettes

Whether or not you are a chain smoker, it is essential to do an exercise that heightens your awareness of bodily processes because as a habitual smoker you've become deadened to and cut off from your insides to an alarming extent. If you want to prove this to yourself, and you should, take the time *now* to remember the first time you smoked and began to inhale. Virtually 100 percent of all smokers had periods of dizziness, nausea (even vomiting), coughing, headaches, and the like when they started smoking—were, in fact, made *literally sick by smoking.* The body reacted violently to the poisons being introduced.

Don't you remember those times? In order to teach yourself to become a smoker, you had to overcome enormous physical resistance and virtually beat your body into submission. After a while, if you do not pay heed to the messages the body is giving you when it is under great stress and in need of help, it stops sending the conscious part of your mind messages at all: the Robot Smoker has taken control. This is happening at the same time that a biological adaptation is going on within you. Your organs are learning how to "survive" in a polluted environment, just as certain freshwater fish, after a time, may learn how to "survive" in polluted rivers, or saltwater fish in polluted oceans, though always with a greater early mortality rate, a higher mutation rate, a shorter life span, or some other destructive consequence.

The Second Cutback

If you had the "will power" to overcome your body's violent resistance to *becoming* a smoker, you have more than enough to overcome the resistance to quitting, and you must find it and bring it to life again. Don't let your R.S. keep telling your Self that you can't. Consider that when you entertain the thought or express the idea that you don't have the "will power" to quit, it is the Robot Smoker playing another clever game of negative Self-hypnosis, and as we saw earlier in the analysis of the (Disad)-Vantage ad, the cigarette companies know this game and exploit it to the hilt (with the sword buried in your body). Don't fall for it. Just keep working, keep hanging in there.

An ad I saw this past February was captioned: "Max wants to be your Valentine." It went on to say, [it has] ". . . a long, lean look you just can't help falling in love with." If this sounds sexy, it is certainly no accident. Sex sells cigarettes. Don't fall in love with death in a slick package. The heart in this Valentine's day message is diseased and failing, but your heart will be getting stronger and healthier because this week you will be cutting down by an additional one-third of your original smoking habit, so that you will be smoking only one-third as many cigarettes as you did when you started the program.

Most people, though by no means all, experience some temporary psychological and physical discomfort when they cut back on their smoking. It is as if the addicted part were being ousted from its control over the Self and were protesting this change. The length and strength of these "protests" will vary from person to person, but remember two vital truths:

1. The protest is *always temporary:* it will not last beyond a certain time frame, and usually a modest one at that.

2. You forcibly overcame the resistance of your healthy Self when you began to smoke or inhale, so there is *every reason to believe that you have the power to quit smoking,* every reason to believe you will overcome the addicted part, the Robot Smoker.

SELF ALLIANCE

To support the Self with helpful and healing procedures is an effective way to further increase its power over the Robot Smoker. It is useful to see the process of quitting smoking as a war consisting of many separate battles between the two forces. Your job is to stay allied to the Self, keeping it well supplied with what it needs in order to keep the fight going in its favor so that the ultimate defeat of the R.S. is assured.

If you are among those for whom reducing your cigarette consumption causes a fair amount of temporary discomfort, and I believe that this includes most heavy or longtime smokers, you will find particular help and ease by using the following techniques which have been designed to minimize these withdrawal effects. In any case, use them *whether or not* you have withdrawal effects; you'll find them to be quite comforting and pleasant.

Since by this week you will have so substantially reduced the number of cigarettes you smoke, you will very likely have a craving for one from time to time when you have decided *not* to yield to the nagging demands of the Robot Smoker. Choose from among the following allies to the Self whenever you decide to resist smoking a cigarette. Use these allies as a substitute, or as a means to get through the period of craving, a period which most often lasts only a brief time. Be sure to use *all* of them at one time or another—don't limit your allies in your battles with the Robot Smoker.

The Allies

RELAXATION BREATHING

Smoking seems pleasurable to some people partially because it involves the act of rhythmic deep breathing (albeit of poisonous gases and particles). Deep inhalation and exhalation is a relaxing activity for all of us. It is related to sighing when we are feeling troubled or anxious—it relieves us by breaking the tension connected with these states.

Why not use the deep breathing alone, without the smoke, to help you relax? Try this exercise *now:*

Sit down on a chair, legs uncrossed, feet on the floor, hands in your lap, spine straight but relaxed. Take a long, deep breath through your nose, mouth closed, until your rib cage and chest are fully expanded with air. Hold your breath for about 10 seconds and then exhale exclusively through your mouth, all at once, allowing your chest to relax abruptly with a sigh. Let 10 seconds pass, then repeat the breathing pattern; after another 10 seconds do it a third time. Wait about 30 seconds and then repeat the entire cycle of three relaxation breaths. Two or three cycles should produce the desired effects, though one is often sufficient.

Do the relaxation breathing exercise while sitting because it may make you feel slightly light-headed for a few seconds, a result of the enriched supply of oxygen to your brain.

Pay attention to how much more relaxed you feel after this exercise. Enjoy your relaxation without a cigarette—an opportunity to weaken the hypnotic bond between smoking and relaxation.

Cigarettes never relaxed anyone by themselves. Relaxation should have nothing to do with smoking. Disconnect those linkages!

RELAXATION IMAGERY

This ally will stand you in good stead, particularly if you feel jittery or tense from time to time (all temporary, remember) as you withdraw from cigarettes. Try combining it with relaxation breathing.

Get to a quiet spot, sit as still as you can with your eyes closed, and try to picture an idyllic scene, one you have personally experienced (e.g., sitting on the bank of a river and watching it flow gently by; or Sunday morning, breakfast in bed and the Sunday paper; or lying on a hillside, watching white clouds adrift against a blue sky).

Envision a relaxing scene of your choice for at least several minutes as many times as you care to each day. You will soon feel calmer and more peaceful inside. The images will become clearer and more effective the more you practice using them. Relaxation imagery can be a refreshing interlude in the day even after you have stopped being a smoker.

Don't be overly concerned if you are among those people

who have temporary difficulty getting to sleep during your withdrawal from cigarettes—your ability to sleep will return, and probably better than ever. Cut down on coffee toward the end of the day, and as you lie in bed at night practice relaxation imagery time and again; it will help to lull you to sleep. Any of the standard sleep-inducing treatments that work for you should be used (but no barbiturates or other chemicals) if and when you need them: a glass of warm milk before bed, sleeping in a cool room, counting sheep, eating a piece of garlic, taking a warm bath.

If by chance you aren't able to fall asleep after a reasonable period of time, don't continue to toss and turn in bed; get up and enjoy the quiet and stillness of the night for a while. Read a book or a magazine, have a hot cup of bouillon or a piece of fruit, listen to some soothing music, write that letter you've been meaning to get to. Make the night pleasant for yourself, make being awake a positive experience. You'll sleep when you're ready to if you don't force yourself.

Don't make temporary sleeplessness into an excuse for not keeping on with the program. It may be a week or, in some cases, a month or more before your sleep pattern fully returns to normal. Bear with it. Take naps, if you can, to supplement the night's sleep.

THE PACIFIER

Oral cravings often increase when we are feeling anxious. Frequently we find ourselves eating more at these times even though we are not really hungry. Occupying the mouth diverts attention from elsewhere and binds nervous energy. We most often associate the mouth with the ingestion of food, but we don't have to eat in order to reduce tension orally, nor do we have to smoke. For some people the act of putting a cigarette into the mouth and drawing on it is much like a pacifier is to a baby—the oral involvement acts as a calmative or a comforter. The movement involving the mouth is often rhythmic, and rhythmical activities are relaxing. Because the act of sucking is primordially related to the most peaceful and contented time, the time of being safe, close to a warm breast, being cuddled, being nourished, wanting something to suck on is perfectly natural at times for all of us and is most common when we are feeling tense.

Yet the chemicals in cigarette smoke, as I noted before, are anything but relaxants—they have a stimulating or antirelaxing effect. It is perfectly fine to want a pacifier if you are an adult—in one form or another they are probably found in all countries and cultures of the world.

But why not use a pacifier that is not harmful and not fattening; that is pleasant tasting; that lasts quite a while; that you can manipulate with your mouth; that is inexpensive and convenient and leaves a pleasant scent on your breath; that is pungent and even slightly anesthetic to the tissues inside your mouth (it can be used to ease the pain of an aching tooth): a whole clove. That's right, an ordinary clove. Just go to the spice section of your local market and pick up a box or two of *whole* cloves. Get the best cloves available; they taste better, and you're going to be using quite a few of them in the months to come. Carry a supply of them with you each day from now on. Whenever you decide to *not* smoke, pop a clove into your mouth. Suck on it, play with it with your tongue, taste the pungent clove oil as it mixes with the saliva, smell the delightful aroma of your own breath—it sure beats a cigarette!

Incidentally, it's nice to have an attractive dispenser that you can keep the cloves in so that taking one is actually a pleasant ritual, as taking a cigarette from the pack is a ritual, or striking a match or flicking your lighter is a ritual. Pacifying manual rituals are also practiced in many countries of the world—the Greeks have their worry beads, some people carry a smooth stone or piece of wood, a "feely," in their pocket; even rosary beads, of course, involve a manual ritual that is pacifying.

I recall my uncle's Sen-Sen dispenser, a thin, silver box that he loved to take out, slide back the little lever, and dispense two or three squares of the licorice candy into his palm or mine. This memory leads me to another point: obviously you don't have to use cloves as your only substitute oral gratification or pacifier; stick cinnamon broken into small pieces, cut-up pieces of ginger, sugarless gum (better for your teeth than gum with sugar in it), Sen-Sen, a toothpick, even a smooth pebble that you suck on for a time—it doesn't necessarily have to be a food substance—can suit the same purpose. You may find a substance on this list or one of your own choosing that you personally enjoy and that works well for you. Use it at times instead of a clove, by all means. Whatever you use should have few or no calories and contain no harmful chemicals, such as alcohol. Use a manual as well as an oral pacifier: the more resources you have, the better.

PHYSICAL EXERCISE

"I can't stop smoking—coughing is the only exercise I get."
L.H., a former client

Physical exercise is one of the most important factors in a successful stop-smoking program for a number of reasons, yet it is often entirely overlooked. This is a lamentable oversight, since physical exercise is one of the most useful and potent allies at your disposal. If you are already a person who has built regular exercise into your life, you are aware of the wide-ranging benefits you receive from it, how well you can feel because of it.

If you are not a regular exerciser, however, you aren't aware of how beneficial it can be to your sense of well-being and to your health. You may have certain prejudices against exercise: it's too hard, it's too boring, your body is just too weak or uncoordinated, you're too old, or whatever. Perhaps in the past you've made attempts to exercise but gave up, got discouraged. You needn't worry if you seem to belong to this latter category because there are ways of overcoming this discouragement.

If you pay careful attention to what is said here and are sure to carry it out responsibly you can become an exerciser with surprising ease, no matter what your past experience has been. Consider this to be a long-range project, one that might take even a year or so to develop fully. Give your Self time to get used to the habit of exercise.

Aside from time, learning to exercise is a matter of decision making and of overcoming inertia; once you've begun to do it regularly, it requires less effort to keep it going. The four factors that help these processes along so that exercise becomes a well-established part of your life are:

1. Start small.
2. Progress slowly.
3. Have fun.
4. Keep the momentum going.

You can increase the amount of exercise you do just by deciding to walk that flight of stairs rather than take the elevator, by deciding to park the car a block or two away from your destination and walk the rest of the way, by getting off the bus one or two stops before or after your destination, or by going for a short walk after work. Of course, if you prefer, whenever you have the time during the day you can run in place, do jumping jacks, arm lifts, knee bends, sit-ups, push-ups, or any other exercise you would care to do.

If you've been meaning to take up a particular exercise or sport or discipline—tennis, running, jumping rope, calisthenics, bicycling, aikido—but just haven't gotten around to it, now is the time to begin. But you must begin modestly. Until you are a nonsmoker, exercise is an ally and not the primary goal; the primary goal at this time of your life is to quit smoking: first things first.

This would be a good week to buy that tennis racquet or those running shoes or to join that gym or exercise class, but I want to underscore the fact that if you set your initial goals too high you can weaken your confidence just when you should be having experiences to strengthen your confidence. Start slowly, gradually. Always keep your exercise goal somewhat *less* than what you are sure you can do. You will begin to build your capacity for exercise almost before you know it. Don't increase the level of exercise until you are easily and regularly accomplishing the level you are on at present—even if weeks pass before the next level can be attempted.

Associate whatever exercise you do with having fun: get yourself whatever equipment you need (don't buy anything too expensive until you're sure that you're going to be making use of it often). Keep records of how many stairs you climbed, how many sit-ups you did, how far you walked. Walk to different places that you've wanted to explore. Vary the forms of exercise you do or vary the way you do your main exercise. Get a partner to exercise with you. Keep experimenting with the many different ways of informal and formal exercise until you find one or more that suit you, that are fun and make you feel good. Keep yourself entertained when exercising: it is the key to having this ally available. Exercise to music if you'd like. And *don't let a day go by without doing some deliberate physical exercise.* Keep your momentum from flagging. It takes far less effort to keep a process going once you have begun it than it does to start from scratch each time.

Aside from simply feeling better, there are a number of other reasons why you *must* include this ally in your repertoire. Deliberate physical exercise is not likely to have become an area conditioned to cigarettes; it is not a link in the smoking chain that is throttling you. In essence, your Self has great power in this area while the Robot Smoker has little or none. Notice that when you feel a craving for or are smoking a cigarette you are not at all likely to be involved at that moment in deliberate physical exercise. You would be made terribly uncomfortable if you did do any exercise while smoking since exercise causes an increased need for oxygen and cigarette smoke crowds out oxygen. Exercise is also helpful because it helps the body get rid of impurities at a faster rate, and as a smoker your body contains inordinate amounts of these impurities.

After exercising, however, you may very well find that you crave a cigarette. Sports and exercise have been heavily exploited by the media (it's hard to find anything that hasn't been). Lots of ads have infiltrated your unconscious which showed professional athletes or "just plain folks like you and me" holding sporting equipment, or wearing clothing associated with one or another sport, having a smoke after their workouts.

Additionally, if you are among those who are concerned about weight gain, studies have shown that, contrary to what has been generally believed, regular exercise *lessens* the desire to eat: it does *not* increase your appetite; it tends to decrease it. Exercise, therefore, helps control your weight in two ways: by burning up more calories and by keeping your appetite in check.

Physical exercise is one of the basic ways to improve health, whereas smoking is one of the basic ways to destroy it. If you have any medical problem, such as heart disease, by all means consult your physician before starting to exercise; otherwise, today is the day to begin. Take a moment now— what will you do to begin? Do not overexert yourself, but make exercise part of your daily routine.

BLOCKADING

With this technique your Self builds a psychological barrier or blockade against the "message" or impulse to smoke a cigarette until the impulse dies down. The ally of blockading is *always* available to you no matter where you are or in what circumstances. Blockading consists of performing a simple mental function whenever an impulse (thought or feeling) to smoke occurs and you choose to resist it. Since you are smoking only one-third as many cigarettes this week as you used to before you began this program, there should be many opportunities to practice this technique. As you will recall, the impulse to smoke will last only a short while before it will disappear again. It therefore makes good sense to barricade your Self from the Robot Smoker for this brief period of time.

This healthy form of resistance can be accomplished by having the voice of your Self erect a word or phrase barrier that drowns out the voice of the R.S., that doesn't let it "get through." By rapidly repeating either out loud or beneath your breath a word or phrase that has power to it (a simple word such as "No!" or "Stop!" or a phrase such as "Beat it!" or even a magic word or phrase like the "Shazam!" used in

Captain Marvel comics or a mantra used in meditation) you will tide your Self over the brief attack by the Robot Smoker. Do this, of course, while the urge to smoke is upon you.

Visualizing will heighten the blockading effect and increase its potency. Close your eyes and imagine, as you are repeating your blockading word or phrase, that you are looking at a long, rolling hill in the near distance, its silhouette dark against an evening sky. On the top of this hill, in red neon lights ten stories high, your blockading word or phrase is flashing on and off as you repeat it. Try the visual blockading technique at the same time you use the verbal blockading technique. Practice doing this *now*. If at first you don't succeed in getting a clear image, keep trying until you do; for many people, developing skill in being able to visualize takes a bit of time.

When the impulse to smoke arises, it is going to be strong for only a short time; your use of an ally such as blockading can really be very brief as well: just pick it up and put it down as needed. One of the other ways that blockading works is that it gives you a bit of time away from the pressure of the impulse to smoke, time for distraction to occur. Something else catches your eye, or ear, or mind, and before you know it you have forgotten all about that cigarette for a while—a victory for your Self. Don't be too proud to accept comfort from these allies. You need, and deserve, all the help you can get. And what you are now discovering is that some form of help is always there, always available.

THE UNMASKING GAME

Unmasking ads can be one of the most powerful deterrents to the impulse to smoke. Unmasking can be made into a kind of parlor game played by yourself or with others. Carefully scrutinize a cigarette ad in a magazine or paper and expose as many of its manipulative devices and lies as you can discover. See how many of these hidden elements you can find. While you are doing this, of course, you are simultaneously sharpening your perception and increasing your resistance to the malicious influence of these ads.

Instead of lighting up, *the next time* you feel like reaching for a cigarette, pick up an ad instead and thoroughly unmask it. Notice how it affects your desire to smoke. Use this ally as often as possible.

Coming Alive Again

It is a basic truth that *any* reason for giving up cigarette smoking is reason enough. Since the addiction itself is always destructive to life and therefore wholly unreasonable, a move away from it is necessarily a move toward reason, a life-affirming move. Whenever you choose not to smoke, no matter what your motive is, you have taken a step closer to revitalizing your health and liberating your Self.

It is a well-accepted fact by now that when you stop smoking many harmful processes actually begin to reverse themselves, and others just stop progressing. The body will usually heal if you will only let it, give it a chance. People who have stopped smoking, *no matter how long they were smokers,* have a lower incidence of disease such as chronic bronchitis, heart and vascular diseases, emphysema, and, of course, cancer, than people who continue to smoke.

As I originally wrote this section I discovered that somehow in my own unconscious was the thought that cancer and emphysema were the only incurable diseases associated with smoking. (I mention this in case you have such an erroneous thought in your own mind.) It is very decidedly *not* true that cancer is incurable. It *is* often curable! At present a rather large percentage of cancer is completely curable by medical intervention and this has been the case for quite some time.

If you have cancer now, the R.S. may have told your Self that "I have cancer anyway, so why stop smoking now—at least I'll die 'happy.' " Don't believe it. If you have cancer, you have all the more reason to stop. If you have cancer and think you're going to die anyway, why are you reading this book, a book about coming alive and staying alive? Now that we are beginning to discover that mental and emotional factors can influence the course of cancer, your decision to stop smoking reflects an attitude that can promote healing; it is an investment in your own future.

Don't confuse the voice of your Robot Smoker with the voice of your Self. You are in the process of restoring your Self to its rightful place as the decision maker in your life course. It is a vital and accomplishable task and you must stick with it, however long it takes, however difficult it may be at times.

If you have emphysema, stopping smoking will certainly help to halt the progress of the disease and you will breathe easier both literally and figuratively when you do stop. Your healthy lung tissue will gradually be revitalized after you stop bathing it in smoke; your cough will eventually go away or be reduced as your body begins to heal. In time you will come to feel more energetic—the experience of life flowing back to you.

The fact that the body will heal itself if only you will give it a chance lends powerful support to the idea that there are *no* good arguments for not stopping smoking. The *only* way smoking can be justified is by rationalization—a sophisticated form of lying.

You are not a nonsmoker yet, but this is the last week that you will be a smoker. Becoming a nonsmoker is a matter of breaking an addictive habit, of becoming free of the *desire to smoke,* not only of refusing a cigarette. For most, though not all, people this takes time, but if you are following the program diligently it will take less time to reach this state, a state in which you have experienced a shift in identity, when *you know you are a nonsmoker.*

With a ballpoint pen or marking pen print the words "The Last" in large letters along the length of one of the cigarettes in your current pack. Do this *now.* Do *not* smoke this cigarette until, in the next chapter, you receive instructions from me to do so.

Transfer this cigarette from pack to pack this week, keeping it with you at all times.

Pitfalls

Read the "Pitfalls" sections at the end of Chapters 1 and 2 again. *Now* add a fifth, sixth, and seventh: (5) "It's too uncomfortable to continue with the program—I've gained some weight, or lost some sleep, . . ." etc; (6) "I'm already seriously ill—it's too late;" (7) "I'm doing so well I don't have to do the rest of the program—that's for people who are having trouble, and I'm not—I'll just stop here [and not complete the program or the book]."

Exercises

1. Continue to practice your *daily* visualization of burning your last pack of cigarettes as described in the "Exercises" section of Chapter 1.

2. Continue to unmask ads.

3. Reduce your daily intake of cigarettes by another third.

This week, therefore, you will be smoking only one-third as many cigarettes as you did before you began the program. Start out each day with *only* this number in your pack.

4. Continue to wrap your cigarettes as described in Chapter 2.

5. Continue to save money in the Health Bank for each cigarette less than the number you smoked before you began this program.

6. Continue to smoke the "anticigarette" brand.

7. Continue using delay periods before each cigarette and occasionally before taking the next drag.

8. Don't smoke in the "knee jerk" area you selected in Chapter 2. Select one other such area this week and don't smoke there either.

9. Continue to examine your rationalizations. Write them down. Think about the "loopholes" in them.

10. Two or three times this week light and smoke a whole cigarette with your eyes closed while breathing through your mouth. Pay attention to how much less "pleasurable" it is.

11. Two times this week sit down, face a blank wall, and in a rather rapid fashion smoke *two* cigarettes, one directly after the other in the exact manner described earlier in this chapter. Pay careful attention to the changes in your bodily processes as you do so.

12. Continue to weigh yourself daily and chart it.

13. Use the "allies" as liberally as possible. Where necessary, reread the descriptions of them given earlier in this chapter:

• Relaxation breathing.

• Relaxation imagery.

• The pacifiers(s), especially whole cloves and a "feely" as well. Carry them with you at *all* times.

• Physical exercise (start small, go slowly, have fun, keep up your momentum).

· Blockading, with and without visualization.

· The unmasking game.

· Other allies you have adapted for your own use.

14. Mark "The Last" on one cigarette. Don't smoke it, but transfer it from pack to pack.

15. If you have extra packs of cigarettes at home, use them up. Buy only one pack at a time this week.

16. Reread the "Pitfalls" and the "Exercises" sections of this chapter *once each day.*

Wait exactly one week before you begin the next chapter, and . . .

PRACTICE WHAT YOU'VE LEARNED.
SLOW OR NO PROGRESS WITHOUT IT.

4

✌

Senior—Graduation

IMPORTANT NOTE: This chapter must be read only at *home*, indoors. Do not read it until you are there, even if it means a short delay. If you are traveling, you may consider your temporary residence as "home."

This is the week you've been preparing for, the week you quit smoking forever. For some of you it will feel like a great relief finally to be finished with this ridiculous habit, and for others it may be a bit scary. Some of you, therefore, will approach the week with eagerness and others with reluctance. The more frightened or hesitant you are, the more you must make use of the "allies." Remember, this program is deeply concerned with bolstering and supporting the Self; if your Self feels uncertain, you must nurture and comfort it just as you would a child who expressed a fear of the unfamiliar. This Self in many ways *is* like a child: inexperienced (at least for as long as you've been hooked to smoking) in how to be a non-smoker. Be good to your Self. Love your Self. Begin by imagining yourself, in the usual way, burning your last pack of cigarettes. Do this *now*, for a few minutes, before you read any further.

Habit Breaking as a Process

Most of the exercises that you practiced during the "Fresh-(wo)man," "Sophomore," and "Junior" phases of the program will be discontinued this week since they are related only to smokers, and in a short time you will have graduated to the status of a nonsmoker. That's right: you should soon, very soon, begin consciously thinking of yourself, calling yourself, identifying yourself, as a nonsmoker; that is, after all, what you'll be.

It will take some time for you to complete this change in your identity and it will probably be even longer before you are wholly and genuinely comfortable with it, but it *will* happen if you follow the program carefully and patiently. Although in some cases the outward behavior pattern of a habit may be altered or eliminated rather rapidly, the underlying conditioned connections, the very essence and definition of the habit, *always* take considerable time to eliminate.

Habit breaking is a process, not a single event.

At some point in this process you will begin to notice that the principal focus of your energy or attention has begun to shift away from just controlling the outward behavior pattern of wanting to reach for a cigarette and has refocused on the *strengthening* of the nonhabituated, or free, Self. In effect, this is the time when the Self has clearly begun to overpower the addicted Robot Smoker, when the tide has begun to turn. When that time is reached, you will begin to feel lighter in spirit and more relaxed. It is as though you have arrived at a level meadow after a long climb up a mountain: the amount of effort you expend becomes very noticeably reduced, and reducing the effort can only lead to an increase in the level of relaxation. In time your general level of relaxedness as a nonsmoker can be far greater than it was when you were a smoker.

Decontextualizing: A Fresh View of Smoking

When you observe either someone else or yourself smoking, you register the impression as a whole; the cigarette smoking is imbedded in a context—the place, the circumstances, the other cues (auditory, olfactory, visual) that are present are all part of your single impression. But have you ever seen cigarette smoking isolated from its context and analyzed into its components?

Try the following exercise in observation and analysis the next time an opportunity presents itself; this is an exercise in *decontextualizing*, a way of seeing the act of smoking nonhypnotically, a way of increasing your objectivity.

Carefully observe people who smoke. First they reach into a pocket or purse and withdraw a rectangular package from which they remove a thin cylinder. They put one end of this paper-wrapped cylinder to their lips and let it dangle there. Next they strike a match or use a mechanical device to bring a flame to the other end of the cylinder. They suck on the end in their mouth and the ember on the cylinder burns and glows, forming an ash. Dense bluish white smoke can be seen in their mouth as they withdraw the cylinder. And then the smoke disappears—they inhale it deeply into their lungs where it remains for a time until it is exhaled through the mouth and/or nose, often in a pattern. They repeat this act time and time again, flicking the ashes that form occasionally, until the cylinder is fairly well gone, and then they crush it into a receptacle or underfoot. Each time the smoke is exhaled it is a paler shade than it was when it was inhaled, suggesting that less is coming out than was taken in. Some part of the smoke is remaining in the body of the smoker. How bizarre!

Viewed in this decontextualized way, the act of smoking comes to look as absurd as it really is, and the person who is smoking truly does look rather like a robot. Imagine for a moment how the act of smoking a cigarette would look to a person who had never known about cigarettes before.

Smoking "The Last" Cigarette

In the pack of cigarettes currently in your possession is "The Last" cigarette, the one you have been transferring from pack to pack this past week, *the last cigarette you will ever smoke.* You may have been saving it with the thought that you will smoke it in a way that will make it a very special and pleasant event (just what the ad agencies want you to think, of course), an event in which you will act as if you were savoring the joys of a rare, good thing. As we've seen time and again, however, smoking is not a rare, good thing; it is common and destructive in all ways.

If you have been harboring the idea that you are going to smoke "The Last" in a positive, pleasant way (examine your thoughts for a moment *now* to see if this pertains to you), put this book down here and take the time *now* to become aware of why this idea about and attitude toward smoking "The Last" are the exact opposite of what should be the case. It is another example of how mind-controlled you've been. The addicted part of you, the R.S., would like nothing better than to have your last memory of smoking be a positive one. Such a memory could potentially weaken your resolve to remain a nonsmoker in the future. Think about it: it would be very foolish to arrange for the last cigarette you smoked to leave a memory trace that was positive in any way, other than that you felt positively relieved that this was your last cigarette and that you would be free of this damaging and ridiculous habit at last.

Therefore, without waiting a moment longer, NOW, *as you read these very words,* go to the bathroom of your residence (it must have a mirror in it—if it doesn't, bring one with you), and also take your current pack of cigarettes, matches (or your lighter), and some cloves. If you were smoking while reading this, put out your cigarette first. Take this book with you.

Then, once there (you should be in the bathroom as you are reading these very words), take "The Last" from your pack and rewrap the remainder of the pack as usual. If "The Last" is the only cigarette left, rewrap the empty pack. You are about to smoke "The Last" cigarette, the last cigarette of your life. It will be smoked in a deliberately counterhypnotic way so that your last memory will be an ally to your Self, not an ally to the Robot Smoker—part of the philosophy that you need and deserve all the help you can get.

Look at the words, "The Last," printed on the cigarette and repeat them to yourself a few times. Consider what this means—the very last cigarette you will ever smoke. Do this slowly, seriously, with concentration and full awareness; think deeply, calmly. Keep checking to make sure that your attention is sharp and focused on what you are doing, as the Robot Smoker may try to dull or divert your attention in some way. Face a mirror and put "The Last" cigarette in your lips so that the words on it are visible in the mirror, and drop your pack of cigarettes (whether it has 0 or 19 cigarettes left in it) into the empty sink.

Do not go any further. First read the next four paragraphs thoroughly and then carry out their instructions as you read them for the *second* time.

If anyone else is home when you are doing this, be sure to close the bathroom door so that you are entirely alone and undistracted. Next, light "The Last" and with the *same* match light the pack of cigarettes in the sink *(be sure nothing else can catch fire)*. Get a really good blaze going on the pack of cigarettes, using as many additional matches as you need.

Then puff on "The Last" *as fast as you possibly can,* inhaling as usual (do *not* smoke this cigarette at all leisurely), while looking in the mirror and watching the last cigarette go up in smoke, dissolve into ashes.

Alternate looking into the mirror with looking at the burning pack of cigarettes in the sink (relight them as necessary), and as you look back and forth, occasionally look "inward" and see in your mind's eye the image you have previously visualized during the course of the program, the one in which you tossed your last package of cigarettes into a blazing fire. Try to superimpose this image upon the pack burning in the sink.

And when you've puffed away that last cigarette and the pack in the sink is burnt up as well, stub out the butt into the sink, scoop up the whole mess, and flush it down the toilet. Open the window. Wash the sink free of the ashes, thoroughly wash your hands and your face, gargle and wash out your mouth with some cool water or mouthwash, and then brush your teeth.

Follow these instructions *explicitly.* Stay alert!

Nurturing and Protecting the Self

When you were a smoker, a major part of your Self was, in effect, in a state of hypnotic sleep. You've begun to be reawakened; you are "coming to." You've just symbolically washed your Self clean of a dirty habit. Look into the mirror. It's worth a smile if you feel good about yourself, a smile that says "Hello" to your Self, a welcome. Pop a clove into your mouth and leave the bathroom. You won't need your matches or lighter any more. Get rid of them *now* and get out of the habit of carrying them.

This Self is much like an infant—still small, not very strong yet; it needs and will continue to need *nurturance* and *protection* in order to develop healthily and become able to exist on its own without cigarettes. During these and the following weeks, therefore, you should be very good to yourself, practicing Self-nurturance and Self-protection as much as possible.

Nurture your Self by administering pleasant experiences to your body, mind, and soul. Hot baths, good reading, fine music or art, massages, love making, saunas, naps and longer hours of sleep, walks in the countryside, exercises of various kinds, good friends and enjoyable conversation, food and pleasant sensory experiences in general (all in the absence of smoking) will do you a great deal of good. Supply them to your Self in liberal doses (don't overdo the food), especially during the next month or so. Indulge your Self a bit.

While you are nurturing your Self you should also be protecting your Self. Therefore, you should avoid contact as much as possible with smokers and with smoking paraphernalia. Sit in the nonsmoking sections of public places. If there are restaurants where you live that prohibit smoking— and there are a growing number of these—frequent them rather than others; if there are stores which ask that you not smoke on the premises, do your shopping in them. Put away all the ashtrays in your home and ask your guests and the people you live with either not to smoke indoors at all or else not to smoke in the same room you are in. Ask them for their help, their indulgence. Tell them why it is important to you.

Be polite to others who are not as advanced as you are about smoking. Being too harsh or forceful tends to induce people to oppose you and, of course, as it should, it angers them. If you are polite and give an open and truthful explanation such as the following one, you will not be likely to alienate anyone: "I've only recently stopped smoking and I'm working on a program to become free of the habit. Part of the program involves some Self-protection, so could you please not blow smoke in my direction?" (Did you know that even breathing the air in a room where other people are smoking causes your lungs to pick up the pollutants which alter your body chemistry? Studies have shown that you don't have to be a smoker yourself to be harmed by it.)

And remember, when all else fails you can always leave the room yourself after giving a similar explanation. If, after you've mentioned it, people express an interest in the program, you might describe it briefly and share your thoughts and feelings about it. The more people who stop smoking, the better for all living things.

Breaking the Hand-to-Mouth Connection

It is quite likely that years of practice in bringing your hand up to your mouth with a cigarette in it (for most heavy smokers this act has been repeated anywhere from hundreds of thousands to several millions of times!) has caused you to develop a powerful association between that hand and smoking, more powerful than you realize. Breaking the connection between your hand and the act of smoking, therefore, makes good sense. It is almost certainly true that you inadvertently look at your hand more often than people who are long-time nonsmokers.

The following technique will help countercondition you by reminding you *not* to smoke when you glance at your hand. Do this *now* and repeat it each morning for at least the next month or two before you start your day. In letters about one-half inch high, print "I.Q." on the front of the lower joint of the thumb on the hand you used to smoke with. Use a ballpoint pen or fine-pointed marking pen and replace the letters during the day if you happen to wash them off. The "I.Q." should be obvious.

If and when people ask you why you have "I.Q." on your thumb, take the time to explain that it is part of a stop-smoking program you are working on and stands for "I Quit." Once again you are "going public." It helps you when you do so and, incidentally, it may stimulate others to make a decision to stop smoking. You may begin to notice others who have "I.Q." on their thumbs. If you do, ask them how they're doing, give them some support, get some support from them. They are allies, no longer strangers. Enjoy the feeling of camaraderie and share your experiences with others who are kicking the habit, or who have already kicked it. You will not lack for company: an estimated 30 million Americans have quit smoking.

The First Week of Not Smoking

Be modest but be positive about your quitting cigarette smoking when discussing it with others. Don't overinflate your success; remember you haven't kicked the *habit* yet—that takes quite a while—you've just begun becoming a nonsmoker. *Being* a nonsmoker is the result of a *process,* not a single event, and the process takes time. There is ample reason to feel good about yourself, proud of yourself, but there is no reason to brag or to be smug. Take one day at a time and don't set yourself up for a loss by exaggerating.

If you discover any cigarettes, including butts, that you've left somewhere—in ashtrays, your car, home, office, shirt or jacket pocket—throw them out *immediately* upon finding them. Don't give cigarettes away. You do no one a favor by offering such poison.

If you smoke marijuana it probably will be better if you decide to refrain from doing so for at least the next few weeks. There are two reasons for this. First, the act of smoking is obviously quite similar in both cases and can, by force of association, cause you to have difficulty maintaining your resolve not to smoke cigarettes. Second, marijuana tends to loosen controls a bit and you will need to maintain certain controls in order to counter what is still your strong tendency to smoke.

The first week of being a nonsmoker is, of course, the hardest. My advice is to take one moment at a time. Don't worry about the more distant future or waste time by thinking about how "terribly difficult" this is or will be. It does not have to be. If and when your Self becomes temporarily frightened or disheartened or fatigued by these kinds of thoughts, you must understand that it is your Robot Smoker who is talking and trying, as usual, to undermine you: yet another trick of the R. S. which needs to be exposed and analyzed.

You must begin to think of *doing something nurturing and protective* for the Self *at once* if ever you feel momentarily tempted or frightened or disheartened. Don't panic; calm action is the key to getting through these moments. Substitute a noninjurious pleasure or diversion. Use one or more of the "allies." The moment will pass and the pressure will abate. And don't think of having to conquer the smoking *habit*. Instead, at the time negative thoughts occur, if they ever do, think of conquering only the very next desire to smoke. Stay present-oriented, not future- or past-oriented, as much as you can. Stay in the moment.

As time passes your desire to smoke will gradually and surely wane. (For reasons which are not entirely clear, with some people the desire to smoke ceases quite abruptly.) It will decrease both in intensity and in frequency, though not necessarily in a smooth fashion.

A habit is usually broken by degrees, by steps. After having a very little desire to smoke for some days and feeling a sense of relief (perhaps on your way to becoming a bit *too* sure of yourself and therefore complacent), you may suddenly be surprised to find yourself having to fight off, with all the ammunition you've been given in this book, a mad craving for a cigarette.

You've already learned a great deal that you can do about these onslaughts from the Robot Smoker. *Don't wait. Act!*

Charting the Course of Your Progress

Progress can be, and usually is, uneven, as you will probably soon discover—but it is *progress,* and one of the most decisive ways you can know you are on the right road is when you discover this uneven pattern in your own case. It is not a cause for despair; it is a cause for a nod of confirmation: "I'm doing well, and as expected. I'm right on course."

So carry on. Keep moving along that path; don't let a few ruts discourage you. It will get smoother the longer you stay on it.

From now on, for the next month or so, you are to carry a small piece of paper or a 3- by 5-in. card and a pen or pencil with you at *all* times. You will be keeping a simple record of your desire to smoke, and in this way you will be able to show your Self concretely and objectively how you are freeing yourself from the grip of the smoking habit.

Each time you *desire* a cigarette for any reason, put a tally mark on the paper or card where you are charting the course of your increasing freedom from being a slave to cigarettes. You are generating your own personal "Emancipation Proclamation." At the end of each day count the total number of these tally marks and then chart it by marking an "X" at the appropriate cross point on a graph laid out as follows:

Desires to Smoke After "Q" Day

On the graph in Figure 1, for example, the person had 15 "desires" for a cigarette on the first day after "Q" day, 20 on the second day, and 17 on the third day.

You have a stopping pattern which reflects the idiosyncrasies of your particular habit; each person's pattern is

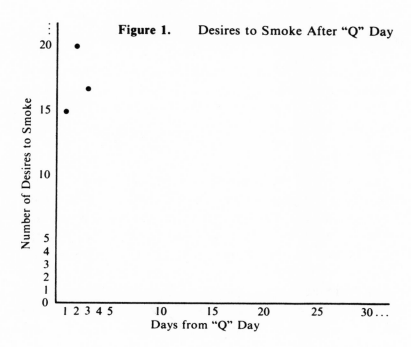

Figure 1.   Desires to Smoke After "Q" Day

somewhat different from the next person's. Nevertheless, there are certain features which tend to be found in nearly everyone's pattern during the course of any consistent effort at habit breaking.

THE HALLMARKS OF HABIT BREAKING

In the paragraphs that follow, some of the most common of these patterns will be described and also plotted on a graph (see Figure 2) so that you can see how they might look. Keep one thing in mind as you look at this graph: it is *not* exactly the way your graph should look; it is only a general example, the kind of chart that would result if you took a sample of, say, 1,000,000 smokers who had stopped smoking with this program and plotted all their patterns combined onto one graph. Some of these features may be prominent on your personal graph and others may be virtually nonexistent, but for many of you, all of them will appear on your graph during the next several weeks.

THE FIRST NEGATIVE SURGE TOWARD SMOKING AGAIN

Though your average daily cigarette consumption before you began the program (called the "baseline") may have been, for example, 23 cigarettes, the frequency of your desire to smoke after you reach "Q" (quitting) day may be, by actual count, *greater* than 23; in other words, you may discover that your desire for a cigarette is temporarily even a bit greater than it was before you began the program. This is illustrated by point A. It is as if the Robot Smoker, or addicted part, recognizing that it is in danger of losing control over your Self, desperately increases its efforts to retain its power. This negative surge won't last very long— hold on and remember to deal with just one urge to smoke at a time. Use all the allies you need. Act!

AVOIDING A FALSE SENSE OF SECURITY: THE PLUNGE

At times your graph may plunge in the opposite direction as well, as illustrated by point B. Shortly after "Q" day you may discover a sudden and rapid reduction in your desire to smoke, so much so that you are in danger of being lulled into a false sense of security, letting down your defenses prematurely. This is one of the danger points you must be on guard against. If you had one good day or more, so much the

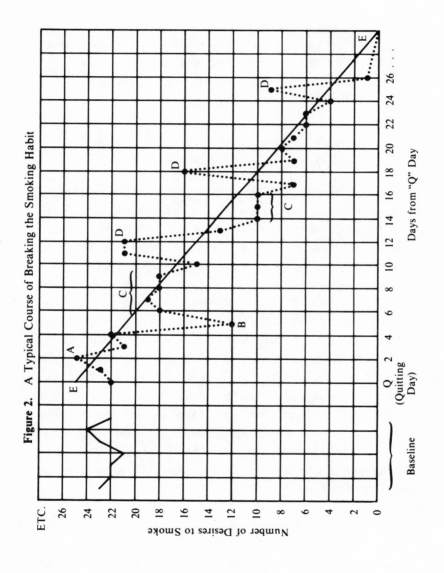

Figure 2. A Typical Course of Breaking the Smoking Habit

better; enjoy this positive experience but remain vigilant and stay right on the program. A great many people owe their former failures in stopping smoking to this false and premature sense of security. Your best defense is to *stay on the program no matter what your chart shows.* You cannot fully eliminate a habit in this short a time. You have not defeated the R.S. just because your graph plunges in the hoped-for direction.

THE PLATEAU: PREPARING FOR THE NEXT IMPROVEMENT

Each additional period of progress in the reduction of your habit (when the line on the graph has made an obvious and fairly consistent drop from its previous level) is quite likely to be followed by a period where, for a time, no *apparent* progress is being made: you are doing all the right things, but still the line charting your desire to smoke is not on the decline. This phenomenon is called a "plateau" (because its shape is fairly flat on top) and is a period of no *apparent* change, which is then *followed by additional change,* as illustrated by points C. During this time the Self is adjusting and adapting to the changes that went before. It is taking a breather and preparing for the next improvement. It is important not to get dismayed at this rest and recuperation phase. Be patient; plateaus are necessary and temporary. They definitely indicate that you are on the right path. You are becoming one with your new Self. *All* growth paths contain plateaus.

ADDITIONAL NEGATIVE SURGES

Additional negative surges are likely to occur from time to time, as at points D. Though it may seem that the sudden urge to smoke has come upon you for no reason at all, just appeared out of the blue, it is in fact *always* triggered by specific causes. The causes are not always immediately obvious, but a careful examination of what has been going on inside and outside you will usually unveil them. Work on finding the reasons for negative surges whenever they arise. Given what you now know about the factors involved in the smoking habit, finding these reasons shouldn't be very hard. Trace back to when the surge began. What were you doing at the time? Where? With whom? What were they doing? How were you feeling? How are you feeling now? What do you need that the desire for a cigarette is a substitute for? How can you go about filling that desire in a *constructive* way? As you examine these surges you will eventually discover that as the time since "Q" day passes, they occur less and less often and also that they generally become less intense when they do occur.

THE TREND LINE: AN ESTIMATE OF PROGRESS

On any single day you may feel either a great desire to smoke or no desire to smoke at all. It would be incorrect, therefore, to judge your progress on the basis of the way you felt on any single day. If you want a visual description of your progress, after you have been keeping the chart for four or five weeks, draw a straight line approximately down the middle of the daily points you have plotted, as the line between points E illustrates. This is known as the "trend," and it is the best way of estimating your progress from a graph. My prediction is that after about four weeks of following the program past "Q" day, the trend will look somewhat like that in the illustration given in Figure 2—a trend toward health and freedom, the slope of the line going in a downward direction, moving toward the absence of having desires to smoke.

It is entirely possible, even highly probable, that the

graph line will bounce back up from time to time after days during which you had no desires to smoke, even after weeks have gone by when no desire to smoke was present. So it goes in almost all cases. Stick with it.

The very best way of knowing your progress will be by the positive changes in the way you feel as more and more time passes since "Q" day was reached.

As you examine your own graph you can learn more about your own smoking habit. Perhaps you notice that all the peak urges to smoke occur on weekends, or that the desire to smoke is at its least on days when you get the most exercise. Learn more about your particular pattern by discovering these "tie-ins." What can you predict about your own habit pattern? Pay attention to your graph in the coming weeks and see if your predictions are borne out. Analyze your habit by using your chart. Learn as much as you can about the way it operates.

The Four RuSes

There are four basic rationalizations at the quitting stage of habit breaking which will need a good deal of your attention and thought for some time to come. I have called these RuSes to indicate that they are, in fact, just that: attempts at Self-deception designed by the Robot Smoker.

These RuSes may be used by the R.S. any time now. Too many people got this far in their previous attempts to stop smoking and got no farther because they followed the lead of a RuSe and didn't recognize that it was the disguised voice of the Robot Smoker. Be on the lookout for these tricky thoughts and their variations and take prompt action against them if and when they appear. Their faulty logic should be analyzed and exposed each time they arise, just as you have been exposing the cigarette ads. Unmask them.

Here are the four basic RuSes and their unmasking:

1. *"What the hell."* In this RuSe the R.S. tells the Self that "Since the air is polluted by industrial wastes. . . ," or, "Since people die early in my family anyway. . . ," or, "Since I could get killed tomorrow by a car. . . ," or "Since I could develop a disease because of atomic testing or chemicals in my food, stopping smoking is irrelevant." Of course, death is an inevitability for all of us, but that doesn't suggest we should do anything to bring it on sooner or increase our chances of falling ill. The healthy Self wants to preserve life and enhance well-being. This RuSe when analyzed is obviously and ridiculously nonsensical. DON'T BUY IT!

2. *"This is 'killing' me."* This RuSe is the same as the fifth "Pitfall" described in Chapter 3. Turn back to Chapter 3 *now* and read that "Pitfall" again in order to refresh your memory. Also in Chapter 3 reread the analysis of temporary discomforts and what to do about them. There is no temporary discomfort that will "kill" you as surely as cigarettes will: "this is 'killing' me" is nonsense based upon a total reversal of the truth. DON'T BUY IT!

3. *"I've got it licked."* Remember the old saying, "Pride goeth before a fall." This is descriptive of a RuSe which usually is used by the Robot Smoker at times when you have been relatively free of the desire to smoke for a while and have been lulled into a false security (as at point B in Figure 2). The rationalization is: "I'm only going to smoke one cigarette (or however many), or take one drag (or more), just to show how it doesn't affect me, how completely I've kicked the habit, how I can put cigarettes away anytime I want to (etc., etc.)." What a line! Ask yourself just what purpose

would be served by engaging in experiments proposed by the Robot Smoker. If you care to demonstrate your "will power," do it in a sane, healthy way: *choose not to smoke no matter what the Robot Smoker suggests.* And beware of letting yourself become smug or complacent about your progress. DON'T BUY IT!

4. *"I didn't want to quit anyway."* Based on the crudest denial of truth, the RuSe tries to suggest that "I only wanted to prove to myself that I could stop anytime I wanted to. Now that I've stopped (for days, weeks, months), I'll start again and stop permanently when I *really* want to." You can recognize a variation of this RuSe in the old comic saying, "Stopping smoking is easy—I've done it dozens of times." DON'T BUY IT!

I want to warn you in advance that these RuSes can come on in force. The pressure on you to "buy" them can be intense. They will seem at times to be perfectly logical and reasonable. They're not—*ever*. Don't forget it. Get a lot of help from your allies and keep unmasking the RuSes as they occur. They are *all and always deceptions* when it comes to the cigarette-smoking habit. Tell someone else, someone close whom you trust and who is supportive of your stopping smoking, about the RuSes as you discover them: the B.S. handed down by the R.S. Once again go public, especially with people who care about you, who are concerned with your welfare, who will help.

Incidentally, you would think that people who are most enthusiastic about your stopping would be, by definition, the people who are closest to you, who care about you. While this is almost always true, there is possibly one major exception: if these people themselves are smokers and aren't quitting, they are more likely to project their negative feelings about themselves onto you. This is basically a form of disguised jealousy or envy. Don't argue with these people—they usually find arguments threatening, and when threatened most people become more entrenched in their positions. All who argue the merits or harmlessness of cigarette smoking are talking insane nonsense; they need sympathetic help in contacting their own sleeping Selves, their own rationalizations. Nonsmokers are the most likely to be supportive and enthusiastic about your decision to quit smoking. Some nonsmokers whom you have been close to, therefore, may have been offended by your smoking, though they may not have said anything about it. They might feel more free to speak now that you have begun to join their ranks, the ranks of nonsmokers. So . . .

Welcome to the ranks of nonsmokers. Have a clove, go for a walk, lie in the sun, get an ice cream cone, take a hot bath, or do all of the above—or do something else that your Self enjoys. Hang in there. For a good many of you, the hardest moments have already occurred.

Unmasking Ads: The Image

The cigarette manufacturers have been pairing smoking with pleasurable experiences since they first began to advertise. What better way to sell their product? Everyone wants more pleasure, and if the public comes to associate pleasure or the good life with cigarettes, the manufacturers have in fact made the association come true: smoking does lead to the good life—*for them,* and for others who make money from the sale of tobacco.

I've rarely met a smoker who deeply recognized the indisputable fact that relaxation and cigarette smoking are themselves physiologically contradictory to each other, not compatible with each other.

Almost everyone who smokes often "relaxes with a

cigarette," takes a "cigarette break," or engages in some other behavior which pairs relaxation with smoking. The more you've repeated this association, the more thoroughly hypnotized or conditioned you've been. And like most hypnotic subjects, you haven't been aware of the hypnosis.

The reason that most smokers think that a cigarette relaxes them, calms them down, has been described in Chapter 1. (Reread rationalization 4, "Cigarettes relax me," in the first chapter *now*, before you read any further.)

Unmasking ads is one of the most effective forms of counterhypnosis.

Open almost any magazine or newspaper these days and you are likely to see more ads for cigarettes than for any other product. In a recent magazine section of the local Sunday paper [1] which contained 47 pages, there were 8 ads for cigarettes! Seven of them were full-page ads and one was a half page; all were in full color, and all of them appeared on odd-numbered pages (I'm not sure of this, but my guess is that odd-numbered pages—the one on your right if you spread a magazine open before you—have been found to be more "noticeable" than the even-numbered pages, perhaps because most people are right-handed and hold the right side of the double page directly in front of them with the left or even-numbered side off to their left). About one-sixth of the magazine was devoted to cigarette ads, 17 percent of its total space!

The conclusion you can draw from this is inescapable: clearly, certain publishing companies can be added to those who profit indirectly from the sales of cigarettes.

So many sources have a powerful vested interest in supporting your smoking habit, and all of them, in one way or another, are putting pressure on you to smoke. You can

1. *California Living* Magazine, *San Francisco Sunday Examiner* and *San Francisco Chronicle,* April 4, 1976.

appreciate the critical necessity of sharpening your awareness of these sources and the processes they use. The more frequently and actively you counterpropagandize against these forces, the easier it will be for you to remain a nonsmoker and the more you will be free of the influence of people who certainly do not have your best interests at heart.

As the times change, the appeal and the images of the ads change. A short time ago when "unisex" (clothes that could be worn by either sex) was the big thing in fashion, cigarette ads with texts that were directed at "a cigarette for the two of you" and showing a "sexy-looking" couple were common, but they aren't nearly so common now.

The most recent trend in cigarette advertising, however, seems to be one in which the emphasis has been put on the numbers game in the low tars derby, and until quite recently the ad agencies hadn't found an appropriate visual image to relate this to, so they relied mostly on the text in order to get their message across (verbal lies instead of pictorial lies).

Each company is trying to cash in on and exploit the latest scientific findings, which suggest that the lower the tars and nicotine in a cigarette, the less harm it is going to do you.

This is hardly revolutionary news. The less junk and poison you put into your body, the better off you are: obvious, and just good old common sense—except, as usual, when you are talking about smoking cigarettes, any suggestion that permits you to smoke and think you are not doing yourself harm simply flies in the face of common sense— always. *Always.*

Here's the catch in the low tars and nicotine game: it centers on the issue of flavor. Since the natural flavoring in tobacco depends largely on various tars and gases, the manufacturers have had to add all sorts of fancy filtering devices to their cigarettes, allegedly to "clean" the smoke of these tars and gases on the way to your mouth, throat, and lungs, while leaving in the flavor. In most instances, new flavoring agents (which are themselves complex chemicals, and, no doubt, toxic) have been added to the tobacco to make up for the flavor removed by the filters.

Merit cigarettes, for example, claim to have "Enriched Flavor tobacco—the new taste technology of smoking." As usual, none of this really makes any sense. Despite the claims made, the smoker does not really benefit because, as I have already mentioned, studies have shown that cigarette addicts who used to smoke a cigarette high in tars and who switched to one low in tars tend to compensate for this changeover. In order to maintain the dosage of tars and nicotine that they were used to, they smoke more puffs per minute than they did originally, or they smoke more cigarettes per day, or they smoke the cigarette further down its length (where the highest concentrations of poisons collect), or they hold the smoke in their lungs for a longer time.[2] In these ways they tend actually to keep their dosage of tars and nicotine way up there.

In essence, you do not derive any benefit from switching unless you simultaneously control all these compensatory factors. Few people do. *Very* few people, in fact. Thus, although the *percentage* of smokers among the general population in the United States is on the decline, those who continue to smoke the new low tars, low nicotine brands have substantially *increased* their average consumption, and the manufacturers are happy—they're selling more cigarettes than ever, over 600 billion last year alone!

It should be borne in mind that the filtering devices themselves have all manner of chemicals in them. The hot gases from the lit cigarette must inevitably transport some of these chemicals to your body as the smoke is inhaled across

2. *Consumer Reports*, May 1976.

them. It is much too soon to know what the long-range consequences of using these flavoring and filtering agents will be. This can be properly evaluated only after many more years have passed, but I believe there is a strong likelihood that the bodily harm and disease produced by the new chemicals in the tobacco additives and in the filters themselves eventually might prove to be even *greater* than the enormous harm caused by smoking unfiltered cigarettes. A recent report [3] has shown that certain of the most harmful, poisonous gases (carbon monoxide, nitrogen oxides, hydrogen cyanide) are found in significantly *greater* amounts in the filter and low tar brands! It may be that filters and low tar cigarettes will add to the very dangers of smoking that they were allegedly designed to reduce!

Somehow, I think the manufacturers are beginning to recognize this. If they have named a cigarette Real and its advertising touts the idea that it is a "natural" cigarette, using no additives, and it shows a picture of two whole tobacco leaves on each pack, and it advertises itself as having a "taste that satisfies," with "nothing artificial added," how far is it from the Camel, Chesterfield, Lucky Strike, and Old Gold of the previous generation—cigarettes that produced all the death and destruction in the first place, that led to the Surgeon General's report and the search for a "safe" cigarette? "You've come a long way, baby," indeed: right back to where you started from—or even further back than that.

Just because the leaf of a plant exists in its "natural" state doesn't mean that it is harmless. There are thousands of plants in their natural states which are deadly when consumed by humans; tobacco is one of them. Don't let those

3. W. S. Ross, "Poison Gases in Your Cigarettes—Part II," *Reader's Digest,* December 1976.

images of large, golden-colored, cured tobacco leaves fool you: those leaves contain deadly poisons. Poisonous mushrooms often have attractive appearances too, but we don't eat them just because they're "natural" or they look good.

The only safe cigarette is one that hasn't been smoked. There will never be a truly harmless cigarette: smoke of any kind, when inhaled regularly over a period of time, especially when it is as concentrated as it is in cigarettes, produces illness and disease. It has always been thus and thus it will always be.

Remember a few years back when Mark Spitz won all those gold medals in the Olympics and his image, as the latest national hero, found its way into the ads? Recall that Camel campaign built around "Meet the Turk. He smokes for Pleasure," showing one of those Mark Spitz look-alikes that we began to see everywhere holding the cigarettes he was advertising (the darkly handsome stranger: mystery, romance, *macho*—a *man*'s kind of cigarette).

In the San Francisco Bay Area several people with creative minds altered the text on these billboards late one night. Talk about unmasking! Instead of billboards greeting you with "Meet the Turk," you read "Meet the Turk-ey" or "Meet the Jurk" or "Meet the Turd." "He smokes for CANCER." Now *that's* truth in advertising!

A few years ago Winston had an ad showing a dark, bearded young man, wearing jeans and a tailored khaki shirt, a comb sticking out of his breast pocket, hair long but neatly combed, so rugged and "natural" looking it must have taken him an hour to get himself to look like that, a chain with a couple of pendants hanging around his neck, radical chic all the way, a guy who is pure media image. He's telling you, in bold type, while looking directly into your eyes, no smile on his lips, an "honest," "direct" face: "If I'm going to smoke, I'm going to do it right." And then he says, this guy who is obviously enormously concerned with his image, "Some people smoke a brand for its image. I don't. You can't taste image. . . ," etc., eventually leading to "Winston is for real."

I'm not even sure what an ad like that is supposed to mean. I guess it's just another appeal to the stereotyped "rugged individualist" from a stereotyped conformist. They've got their concept of reality turned backwards. They're selling confusion, and if you can be confused enough you'll buy anything.

I can't keep from laughing as I read the text and look at the ad before me. I've been unmasking ads for so long now that it has become second nature to me, as it will to you in a short time if you will consciously practice unmasking all the cigarette ads you see. The paradoxical thing about this is that finally cigarettes are giving me pleasure of a sort: I enjoy looking at the ads, and I have fun unmasking all their sneaky components. My family and I play a little game, which my son, Evan, particularly enjoys. It consists of seeing who can find the next component of the ad's "big lie" (whether it is in the wording, the visual images being used, the brand name itself, or elsewhere) and tell what it is supposed to make you think and/or feel, just as I have been doing in this book.

While we are having this fun together, my son, of course, is building his immunity against being influenced by such attempts at brainwashing, and since no one in our family smokes, it is unlikely that he will ever become a smoker. This education is one of the things we feel that we owe him. We feel that our responsibility to help him to develop a smoking immunity is no less than our responsibility to see that he receives polio vaccine. We would no more deliberately increase his chances of becoming a smoker by being smokers ourselves than we would deliberately bring a sample of live polio virus into our house.

If you have children or plan on having children, you might consider these ideas. They will help remind you of how deadly serious the habit of cigarette smoking really is.

MORE ADS, MORE LIES

We've already looked at the naming of cigarettes and the text of the ads, so now let's go back to that magazine section I referred to before and unmask some of the *visual,* nonverbal, manipulations in each of the eight ads.

The first ad, associating cigarettes with humor, is for Benson & Hedges. It is pushing the hard or crush-proof pack by showing a picture of three middle-aged businessmen, exasperated, comic expressions on their faces, all squeezed into the back seat of a car.

Can you imagine being in the back seat of a car with two other people, all of you smoking and not a gas mask within miles? Your lungs are collapsing, but your crush-proof packs? Ah, thank Benson & Hedges, they are intact!

The second ad, associating cigarettes with nature and tranquillity, is for Kool. It shows a magnificent waterfall flowing from one rocky tier to another out of a verdant woods and into a pool at its base.

There are no people in the picture. Why? I imagine it is because a group of smokers set out to hike to the spot for a picnic, but no one had the breath and the stamina to make it. In fact, it looks as if smokers have never visited the place: not a discarded butt, pack of matches, or an empty, crumpled pack of cigarettes to be seen. And the trees are still standing, not burnt down by careless smokers.

A perfect spot for a nonsmoker. You can almost smell the fresh, pine-scented, smoke-free air.

The third ad, associating cigarettes with being fashionable and "in," shows the latest version of the radical chic guy—his image has to be brought up to date every so often because what is trendy and "hip" changes pretty regularly—this time he looks all curly-haired, with a long mustache, no beard, a pendant, and a leather jacket with the sleeves rolled up. He's looking straight at you with those "honest" eyes, and he's coming on with the "Winston is for real" bit. For real what? Disease? Addiction? Conformity? It is about as un-hip as you can get to robotize yourself by smoking, and what person of sound mind would want to live according to the R. J. Reynolds Tobacco Company's definition of reality?

The fourth ad, associating cigarettes with "togetherness," is for Max and uses a unisex, cigarette-for-the-two-of-you appeal. It shows a young couple dressed in similar outfits; both of them are smiling broadly and his arm is around her shoulders as they walk toward the viewer. Naturally, each is holding a cigarette. (The ad also involves a sweepstakes contest.)

But wait, suddenly her smile changes; she begins to cough, only a bit at first, but then more and more. It's becoming uncontrollable. She can't stop. And since what's good for her is what's good for him, he joins her. Pretty soon they're holding hands and coughing together, doubled over, hacking away and spitting up phlegm. Yes, folks, share an experience with the one you love. Remember, Max gives you the hacks!

The fifth is a "low tars" ad based on an appeal to *health* (!!), so it depends mostly on text and name to introduce its lies. In this case we must look again at the ad's language in order to unmask it. It shows two packs of cigarettes, one menthol and one regular, and in small letters it says: "There are many reasons to smoke Now." Catch the double entendre—the cigarettes are called Now and the message is straight hypnotism: "There are many reasons to smoke now." Smoke Now, now—and fall ill later.

The sixth ad, associating cigarettes with sex and romance, is for Eve and shows an attractive woman dressed in a blouse made from the material which has the same design printed on it as the cigarettes and their containers have. She is reclining seductively in front of a blazing fire, holding a cigarette in her hand. Eve, forerunner of all temptresses, waiting in front of that fireplace for her Adam. Irresistible.

Her warm, crimson, slightly parted lips await that first kiss. We approach her. The anticipation is almost more than we can bear. Closer, closer ... until we come to notice the nicotine-stained, yellowing teeth beneath her sensuous half-smile.

Perhaps it's only the lighting. We move closer, approach her face, bend down to kiss her ... and become aware of the sour smell of her breath and the stale, bitter pungency of tobacco smoke lingering in her wavy, auburn hair.

The fire of our passion has begun to diminish, yet we persist. And when our mouth meets hers at last it is suddenly like kissing the bottom of a soft ashtray: rancid and awful.

"Would she settle for just a game of *Monopoly* instead?" we wonder.

The seventh ad, associating cigarettes with being *economical,* is for More and pictures two enormous packs of cigarettes, menthol and regular (notice that all menthol cigarettes are associated with the color green, connecting the idea of menthol with the freshness of nature), shot from the top and looking like tall skyscrapers, the World Trade Towers in New York City. Each pack has a cigarette extending from it, further emphasizing the absurd length of these 120-mm coffin nails. They're brown, as many cigarettes are nowadays—more "natural looking" and "organic," I suppose. Death and disease in a plain brown wrapper—and more of it.

Is your health taking too long to break down because you're smoking regular-sized cigarettes? Why wait any longer? More gives you more puffs per cigarette, speeds things up, puts a swifter end to all that waiting.

The eighth ad is another "low tars" number, a variation on the Vantage ad that was analyzed in Chapter 1, and it, too, depends nearly entirely on written language to manipulate you. There's no need to dwell on what by now should be glaringly obvious.

There you have it: eight ads, seven lies, linking cigarette smoking to humor, nature and tranquillity, being fashionable, togetherness, health, sex and romance, and saving money. Any avenue that can possibly be exploited will be—just the way a good hypnotist works. But in this case no one asked if you minded being hypnotized. And no one is likely to ask the children who read and see these ads if they want to be influenced in these ways, but they will be, just as you were; make no mistake about it.

The Co-Predators and Their Prey

Cigarette manufacturers and advertising firms work side by side; they are co-predators.

A particular target population is selected—say, the emerging independent woman—and then not only is a specific ad campaign designed to capture the "prey," but an entirely new product may actually be created in order to increase the chances of making that capture.

Virginia Slims, Dawn, and Eve were all created to hook women on smoking, and the statistics show that these brands are very effective in doing just that. More women are smoking at present than at any other time in our history—and more women are getting lung cancer than at any other time in our history.

Even as you read this book, other target populations are being zeroed-in upon. Although new *brands* of cigarettes have not yet been specifically created to "capture" these target populations, the advertising campaigns for the already established brands have been modified specifically for this purpose. In predominantly black neighborhoods, therefore, black models appear on the billboards in the hope that black people will begin to think of a particular brand as "their" cigarette, will develop a product identification with a particular brand. This trend is bound to expand—Latin Americans, Orientals, old people—which group will the snare be laid for next?

What is perhaps most horrifying about all this is that adolescents are now being stalked by the unholy alliance of tobacco companies and advertising agencies with all the cunning that they have perfected in their other campaigns. In recent ads I've noticed that the models appear to be very young looking, younger than I've seen before. And in many cases they seem to be engaged in a kind of activity that one tends to associate with the high school years. There are now 4.5 million teenage smokers in the United States—about 30 percent of school-age children smoke!

We all know how easily influenced adolescents are. Most smokers began during their adolescence—the peer pressure to do so can be extreme. Adolescents especially don't need any additional encouragement to smoke; they need more education and support for not smoking than any other group.

A friend of mine reports that all six of his fourteen-year-old daughter's friends smoke! But his daughter doesn't, and she isn't tempted to because she has been brought up in a home where smoking is simply not permitted, even by guests. Her education, in addition, has included much of the material discussed in this book.

The people who live in this home know how to care for their health and are aware of the politics of the tobacco-ad industry partnership (what else would you call it?). They believe that no one should have a right to pollute the air they breathe, and practically the only place left in this country where you can control the pollution of the air is in your own home.

Have you given up this right to clean, uncontaminated air? Don't you want it back? What are you doing in your own home to make this possible? Why wait any longer? It's *your* home, *your* health and the health of *your* family, the air *you* breathe. . . . Do something about it!

Pitfalls

Read the "Pitfalls" sections at the end of Chapters 1, 2, and 3 again, *now*. Then add the four RuSes described in this chapter as Pitfalls 8, 9, 10 and 11, and reread them *now*.

Exercises

1. Continue to unmask ads, but now begin to talk with others about your unmasking, particularly with any children or adolescents with whom you are in contact (if you work with children, you have a unique opportunity and responsibility to do this). Have fun at it.

2. Continue to save money in the "Health Bank" for each cigarette you are now not smoking.

3. Continue to examine your rationalizations. Write them down.

4. Weigh yourself daily or, if you prefer, somewhat less often, and chart it, as you have been doing.

5. Use all the "allies" as liberally as possible. (Reread the "Allies" section of Chapter 3 *now.*) Keep cloves or other allies with you at all times.

6. On a few occasions this week "decontextualize" your

observations of someone who is smoking (see the description earlier in this chapter) and notice how robotlike a smoker really looks.

7. Practice Self-nurturance and Self-protection as described in this chapter.

8. Continue doing your daily physical exercises. If possible, increase them slightly.

9. In pen, put the letters "I.Q." on the thumb of the hand you used to smoke with. Renew the letters as they wear off. They should be clear and present from the time you arise until the time you go to bed. Do this every day.

10. Throw out all cigarettes and butts whenever and wherever you find them. Put away all the paraphernalia of cigarettes: ashtrays, lighters, cigarette cases, etc.

11. Keep a daily tally of "desires to smoke" on a card you carry with you. Transfer these figures at the end of each day onto a graph labeled as in Figure 1. Compare your graph from time to time during the next month or so with the example in Figure 2 and observe the various patterns of your habit-breaking course as they emerge.

12. Be an ally to your Self and watch your health gradually improve. If you should feel in need of additional help of a special kind during this week, you will find it in the next chapter. So, if you are among those who from time to time experience extreme distress as you kick your habit, by all means read the next chapter *before* a week has passed. Otherwise, you may wait the usual week before reading it. It is *not* an optional chapter; it is fundamental to the program and must be read as carefully as all the other chapters were. And . . .

PRACTICE WHAT YOU'VE LEARNED.
SLOW OR NO PROGRESS WITHOUT IT.

5

✿

Graduate School

The hardest part of the journey back into being a nonsmoker will already have taken place for many of you, while for others among you some of the major battles with your waning addiction have yet to be fought. The principal concerns of this chapter, therefore, will be to consolidate and strengthen the gains you've made if you're in the former category, and if you're either partially or wholly in the second category, you will be introduced to one of the most potent weapons that can be used against the R.S. In any case, it isn't much use to categorize yourself; just continue to operate according to the principle that you need all the help you can get and can get all the help you need. Here's more of that help.

The Spoiler

Each additional week you don't smoke increases the likelihood that you will become a lifelong nonsmoker. The most difficult period of all for most people, as you may have supposed, is during the first weeks of abstinence.

But if you happen to be among those people for whom the intense pressure to smoke does not let up rather substantially by the end of the first or second week, don't despair, you are not alone. This is an unmistakable indication that your smoking habit was linked in an extremely powerful way to a wide array of internal and external factors. Perhaps this is the first time you have been made so clearly aware of just how thoroughly you had been hooked to this deadly habit. All the more reason to persist: the one thing you can be absolutely certain of is that the pressure or discomfort *will* let up eventually, and sooner rather than later; most people experience a good deal of relief by the end of the second week after "Q" day. Whenever you feel impatient or anxious or a bit disheartened, you must learn to ask your Self, "What ally can I use to make me feel better?" Above all, *do NOT be passive* in the face of any unpleasant feeling connected to smoking; you must *act*. You must help your Self to the help that is available.

This help can include a technique which is unlike any other used in this program in that it is based upon the principle of punishment rather than the principle of reinforcement. Simply stated, it depends for its effect upon the delivery of an unpleasant stimulus to the Robot Smoker during those moments when it is urging you in an especially strong or persistent manner to smoke; that is, when it is nagging you.

I call this technique "The Spoiler" because it quite effectively spoils the attempts of the Robot Smoker to retain or regain control over the Self. It is a surprisingly simple procedure and, when properly used, can be extremely useful in eliminating even the most powerful instances of the destructive smoking urge.

Get a rubber band (one about ⅛ inch wide is ideally suited for this purpose) that will fit comfortably—not too tightly or too loosely—around your wrist. Put this band on either one of your wrists from day to day. Whenever you get besieged by the urge to smoke and want or need additional help in countering this pressure, snap the band against your wrist by stretching it several inches and then letting it go. Alternate snapping it against either the sides or the inner or outer part of the wrist: Keep snapping it until the desire to smoke abates for at least 15 seconds.

The Robot Smoker is learning that every time it pressures you it is going to get painfully punished until it stops. After a short time it will be sending you urges much less frequently, and when these urges do appear they will be much weaker. Keep your eye on the daily graph you are keeping of "Urges To Smoke" (Figure 2) and watch for the decrease in their frequency. You will probably be able to observe a positive change within several days after beginning to use The Spoiler.

In order for The Spoiler to work, however, you must be sure that the snap of the rubber band:

1. is sufficient to cause *some pain* but not to cut your skin or damage you in any way.

2. is delivered as soon as the nagging impulse to smoke *begins,* and *simultaneously* with it if and when it persists.

3. *continues* until the urge leaves for at least 15 seconds (for *any* reason—even, for example, because you got distracted when the phone began to ring).

As I have already indicated, you will discover before long that the impulse to smoke is not only occurring less frequently, but it is easier to get rid of than ever before. One snap of the rubber band will soon be sufficient to get rid of an urge, though when you first begin to use The Spoiler you may have to snap it many times to beat back the Robot Smoker. After a while, usually within a few weeks, merely glancing at the rubber band will rid you of an urge to smoke. And after an additional period of time you will probably not have to do even that much.

When you see The Spoiler you should plan on using it consistently for a fair period of time (anywhere from one month to several months or more). It should be worn around your wrist from the moment you arise until the moment you retire. It's a good idea to keep a spare rubber band with you at all times in case the one you have breaks or you lose it. Don't be caught unprepared.[1]

Since we are operating according to the concept of "going public" whenever possible, it will mean, of course, that you should use this technique whenever and wherever it is necessary. Saving it for use only when you are alone makes no sense at all. If anyone asks you what you are doing, tell them unembarrassedly that it is a technique you are using as part of a stop-smoking program. Most of the people I've worked with reported that going public about any aspect of quitting smoking brought them a lot of support and encouragement from others.

If you have any fears that others will mock you or that you will be made to feel embarrassed, you almost certainly will soon be over them after you go public. People are generally inclined to be sympathetic to those who are becoming nonsmokers; they know that it often involves a difficult struggle. Other people's interest, encouragement, and support can be among the most useful of all the allies to the Self. Don't avoid this resource. Make your Self available to it: go public.

And incidentally, be honest when others ask you how it was to stop. Don't exaggerate one way or another. Among other things, exaggeration can discourage other people from beginning or continuing their own efforts to stop, and no one should be discouraged from improving his or her health.

---

1. See the "Exercises" section of this chapter for a further description of the continued use of The Spoiler.

Dealing with Gallows Humor

Rare occasions may arise in which someone *does* try to undermine you, usually by making fun of a technique you are using, or taunting you "good-naturedly" by purposely blowing smoke in your direction or insistently "pushing" a cigarette at you. These maneuvers are in reality forms of gallows humor, situations in which something that is essentially very serious and potentially damaging is cloaked in jest, like a snowball with a rock hidden in it tossed at you by someone with a smiling face. But, as Shakespeare knew, the truth is often said in jest: gallows humor is, in effect, a hostile albeit disguised attempt to undermine your efforts.

It is obvious that most people who resort to these maneuvers would like to stop smoking themselves but haven't done so for one reason or another. On the deepest level they usually feel quite bad about themselves, principally angry and guilty. They may be threatened when anyone else is succeeding where they have failed, or they may have feelings of jealousy. They may have wanted to stop smoking themselves, but either they didn't have the confidence to make the decision to do so or they didn't know a method to use, to give them the help they needed.

Although there is no reason to get heavy-handed or angry with such persons, it is important that you do *not* cooperate or collude with their inducements to failure. Do *not* smile back at someone who is tossing gallows humor at you. At the least, look in their eyes with an impassive, "flat" expression on your face, an expression which says, "I don't like your message and I'm not going to pretend that I do." An even better response, however, is one which is more active. In a pleasant but serious manner you might actually say something like, "Please don't do that. I *really am* quitting smoking, and what you just did makes it harder for me." This way of relating can even transform underminers into allies, perhaps to the point where they might be stimulated to begin a stop-smoking program themselves. Fellow "stoppers" often make the best allies.

Some Food for Thought

The strength of a habit's control over you is greater when others whom you are close to are themselves hooked on the habit. The cigarette-for-the-two-of-you ads mentioned earlier have been designed expressly to capitalize on this well-known fact. Two people in the same household who are hooked to cigarettes make it substantially more difficult for either of them to become a nonsmoker. Conversely, the power of any habit-changing program is *increased* when others whom you are close to are themselves involved in the same program or are already free of the habit. Therefore, if at all possible, try to get a partner in this program (it isn't necessary that this partner start at the same time you do), someone with whom you live or work or play. Mutuality is powerful and comforting, the best source of support. And support is something we all need.

The question inevitably arises as to whether smoking pipes or cigars can be used as a substitute for smoking cigarettes. While it is true, so far as we can determine, that both cigars and pipes seem to cause less physical harm than cigarettes do because the smoke from them is usually not inhaled, people who try to substitute cigar and pipe smoking for their cigarette habits *almost always* end up smoking cigarettes again. That is a compelling fact and you should heed it. Also, bear in mind that a higher incidence of cancer of the mouth and lips is found among habitual pipe and cigar smokers than among cigarette smokers, and pipe and cigar smoke may pollute the air even more than cigarette smoke does. For the most practical of reasons, therefore, don't *substitute*. You are virtually begging for failure if you do.

Over the years I've observed that many ex–cigarette smokers have become the most vocal proselytizers for nonsmoking. After a period of time cigarette smoke becomes particularly offensive to them: their sense of smell has fully returned and they are able to recognize for the first time in a long while just how foul the reek of cigarette smoke is, how it lingers on things long after the last cigarette has been smoked, how stale smelling the odor of crushed cigarettes is in an ashtray, how much more pleasant other fragrances can be (clean air, lilacs, fresh-baked bread).

I do not think that most people become advocates of nonsmoking for altruistic reasons; I think their advocacy is usually a form of enlightened self-interest. They simply want to have the right to breathe clean, healthy air. And what could be a more fundamental and reasonable right for all of us?

Breathing clean air is one of the most basic rights of all living things. It should be guaranteed and protected by the government, just as the rights of free speech, free press, and free assemblage are. At the very least, there should be a law requiring that all public gathering places have nonsmoking sections; it is more logical, however, to ban smoking entirely from such places.

Laws protecting the right of people to breathe clean air are finally being drafted and passed by more and more state legislatures. I predict that as nonsmokers become increasingly vocal about their rights, such laws will come to be the rule rather than the exception. The government should resume its involvement in antismoking advertising, reviving as a model the antismoking campaign it made on T.V. in the late 1960s. But the ad campaigns should be even more skillful and pervasive; they should be as compelling and eye-catching and clever in presenting the truth as the cigarette companies' ads are in spreading their lies. The ad campaigns should involve billboards along the highways and in the cities, ads on radio and T.V., in newspapers and magazines, exposing the dangers of smoking. And this advertising campaign should be paid for entirely out of revenues from a tax on the sale of tobacco products.

To follow the most logical course, however, the government should, in addition, completely ban the advertising of tobacco products; other countries have already moved in this direction. And it most certainly should stop subsidizing tobacco farmers (currently at a total of some $60 million a year) for growing a disease-producing, nonedible crop on lands that could potentially grow nutritional foods to help feed the millions of hungry people throughout our country and the rest of the world.

Since the government has taken no strong action banning cigarette advertising, except on radio and T.V., I have noticed in recent months that some people in the San Francisco Bay Area have begun a kind of campaign of their own. Several billboards advertising various brands of cigarettes now have the word CANCER added in large letters printed diagonally across their entire surfaces in a contrasting color paint.

An ingenious solution really, since it finally makes the ads *true,* and as it does so it promotes the public welfare instead of undermining it. It elevates the consciousness of smoker and nonsmoker alike, of anyone who happens to look at that sign. And, perhaps most importantly, children,

the most easily influenced of us all, as soon as they are able
to read are given education for their health, not encouragement for their harm. I have never met a smoker who would
like his or her children to smoke. Would you like your
children to smoke? All cigarette advertising increases the
likelihood that children who see it will become smokers. It is
something to think about—something to do something about.

I don't intend to flood you with a mass of data concerning
the various aspects of smoking and health, but I do think you
should be aware of some of the more compelling of these
facts, many of which you may not have heard about before.
I've included a number of them at the end of the last chapter
in the book. Read them at your leisure, *but read them.*

Speaking of facts, wouldn't Fact be a great name for a
cigarette? The name could help to convince the public that
the text of the ad promoting it was factual. This might act as
a reassurance to them and lead them to smoke Fact in
preference to other cigarettes. And the appeal would be to
something new, not the low tar and nicotine bit. ("Tar" is
often put in quotes in cigarette ads because there are really
many tars, not just one. There are over 1500 chemical
compounds in these tars!) An appeal, for example, to low
gas, low "tar" (after all, smoke is mostly gas) with a text
something like:

> Chances are, you've never heard gas and cigarettes
> mentioned together before. Just "tar" and nicotine.
> According to some critics of smoking, gases are part of
> the controversy too. You see smoke is mostly gas. And
> despite what we tobacco people think, these critics say
> it's just as important to cut down on some of the gases
> as it is to lower "tar" and nicotine. No ordinary
> cigarette can do it. But Fact can. Fact is unique, the

first cigarette with a revolutionary Purite [that would be another perfect name] filter. And Fact reduces gas . . . , etc.

Pretty far-fetched stuff, but, of course, Fact is a real cigarette, introduced on the market when I began writing this chapter, and the text above is a verbatim quote (except for my parenthetical comment) from an ad for it. An ad about gas—and did you ever hear such gas, so much hot air in your life? Such flatulence, such pure, unadulterated B.S.?

It is actually getting difficult to invent an ad using a concept that will appeal to many people which hasn't already been exploited by someone in the cigarette industry. But, how about Relaxies [2]—the cigarette that soothes the nerves of a person on the go, that lets you sleep; the cigarette with Tranquileze, the gentle tranquilizer. Or Machos—Tired of all those light, dainty smokes? Need a cigarette with punch—a man's cigarette? Or Intellect—the cigarette for the thinking person, for those of us who are not satisfied with easy answers. Or Orgasmo—Put fun in your life and make smoking a peak experience. Suck on an Orgasmo. Or Guys n' Dolls—A cigarette for the two of you, that tells the world how much you mean to each other. The cigarette of love. Or Power—For the person at the top—or on the way to it.

It wouldn't surprise me if some of these very names or concepts were eventually used by the ad agency–tobacco industry alliance. If it is possible to name a cigarette True and not tell any of the truth in advertising for it, if it is possible to call a cigarette Fact and give no facts in its advertisements, it should even be possible to call a cigarette Health, though what any cigarette really promotes is disease!

2. It almost sounds like marijuana, but that's already been "invented" by nature, used in parts of the world for thousands of years, and not in need of being reinvented.

Where certain big businesses are concerned, making money has become the only value and they will go to any extreme to make it, including the marketing of illness and death in a disguised form: the cigarette, regular or extra long, brown wrapper or white, filter or nonfilter.

Your personal campaign of keeping your Self counterpropagandized against ads for cigarettes, however you choose to do this, is a fundamental part of remaining a nonsmoker. The odds are going against you if you don't stay alert to doing this every chance you get.

Advertising works. It is based upon sound principles of altering people's behavior. It promotes a kind of mass hypnosis, and you are being bombarded with it and influenced by it everywhere you turn. More cigarettes are being smoked in the United States than ever before and, as I have already noted, since women have been specifically targeted by the ad agencies, their death rate from lung cancer has gone up alarmingly. The American Cancer Society reports that lung cancer among women has doubled in the past ten years, though at one time lung cancer was only about one-sixth as common among women as it was among men. At one time, of course, many fewer women smoked than men. A large part (in my opinion, the *largest* part) of the increase in number of women smokers *must* have to do with advertising.

Over $300 million is spent each year to advertise cigarettes. The manufacturers know full well that once they've got you hooked on nicotine you are very likely to become an addict, and their customer, for life. They make their living from your addiction: legalized dope pushers. They're so motivated to hook you that they'll even pass out free cigarettes on the street corner (just like some pushers of heroin do at first), at the market, even on college campuses. Having a college education certainly doesn't make you immune to their influence. Keep your Self uninfluenced by people whose only concern is to robotize you in order to serve their own economic ends. Counterpropagandize, counterhypnotize, by unmasking ads every chance you get. After a while you will not only make your Self immune to the influence of cigarette ads, but each unmasked ad will become a reinforcement for not smoking.

And, no matter how you look at it, the point remains the same: there is *no way* you can smoke safely. Your only chance is to give up the habit entirely. The basic truth as far as cigarettes are concerned is: the fewer you smoke, of any kind, the better off you'll be. And you'll be best off, naturally, if you smoke none.

You'll find yourself in good company, for even though the total national consumption of cigarettes is higher than ever, during the past ten years the percentage of the population who smoke has been decisively on the decline. A recent survey showed that over 50 percent of American men were cigarette smokers in 1966 but only 39 percent smoked in 1975. In the mid-1960s about 32 percent of American women smoked and then this increased to 42 percent by 1970 (when ad campaigns were most heavily directed at capturing the female market), but it was down to 29 percent in 1975. Fewer people are smoking but those who continue are smoking greater quantities of cigarettes than ever.

A new social movement has already been launched, a movement that actively promotes the right of nonsmokers to breathe fresh air, and it is picking up momentum and gaining influence very rapidly. So far about twenty states already have laws restricting public smoking, and if this trend continues, before long all states will have such laws. In Italy a law has recently been passed that does not stop at merely restricting smoking in nearly all public places; it bans smoking in these places entirely. I've been in movie theaters where a large part of the audience has cheered and applauded when a sign announcing no smoking was flashed on the screen.

In October, 1977, the Surgeon General of the United States, Dr. Julius Richmond, proposed a National Don't Smoke Day. The government is finally getting more deeply committed to doing something about this menace to public health.

Sources of Self-Help

Even though there will probably be moments in the future when you experience a surge of pressure from the Robot Smoker (illustrated as points D in Figure 2), *not* smoking will most certainly become more and more natural to you as time passes. Be patient and keep working. The day is not far away when you will notice how much easier it has become not to smoke; or has that day already occurred?

In the event that you are pressured by the R.S. and have a sudden urge to smoke at any time in the future, there is a great deal you can do to get rid of it. Here are some possibilities. Use as many of them as you need:

1. *Analyze its source.* Why did the urge occur when it did? What or who triggered it? What associations were activated? Did you have a visit from an old friend who came to town and with whom you smoked when you were in college? Were you feeling angry or tense or frustrated because of something that happened or didn't happen? Were you really just bored? Did someone else near you light up, or someone in the film you saw? Did you see an ad for cigarettes that you didn't unmask? Are you trying to look a certain way or feel a certain way, a way that you have associated with smoking a cigarette?

2. *What RuSe is accompanying it?* What rationalization is

your Robot Smoker suggesting that you use? Check your "reasoning" against the list of RuSes in Chapter 4.

3. *What do you want that a cigarette is a substitute for?* Were you really hungry or thirsty or tired instead? What healthy way can you find to comfort or support your Self? What harmless substitutes can you make use of? And if you can't get what you'd like directly or at the moment, either do without it or delay doing anything about it until it *is* possible to get.

4. *Which allies can you make use of?* Use The Spoiler. Unmask an ad. Use as many allies as you need. Leave where you are. Do something else, somewhere else; alter your immediate context.

Above all, remember that time is definitely on your side in this project of Self-improvement. *If and when an urge comes upon you, by now even a simple decision to delay doing anything about it for 5 minutes or so while using The Spoiler will usually lead to the urge disappearing entirely.*

If you have been following the program diligently, your smoking habit is very much weaker than it was and growing more so every day—and the power of your healthy Self is simultaneously increasing.

Pitfalls

Follow the directions given in the "Pitfalls" section of Chapter 4. Reread them *now*. And for the next month or so reread them a few times each week. They will keep you reminded of basic concepts that, at this early stage, you are still apt to forget. The Robot Smoker has not yet been fully eliminated and won't be for some time to come.

Exercises

The exercises this week consist of *repeating all* the exercises given last week. Then add the following:

1. Use The Spoiler for the next two weeks exactly as it was described earlier in this chapter, after which you are to change your technique as follows: starting two weeks from now, instead of snapping the rubber band against your wrist *each* time you feel the urge to smoke, snap it only *every other* time (in other words, do not use The Spoiler more than 50 percent of the time you are dealing with the urge to smoke). If and when urges arise, deal with them in other ways: use diversions, substitutes, anything that works.

After two weeks at this 50 percent level, begin to snap the rubber band on a random or intermittent basis, no longer in any consistent fashion. The reason for this alteration in schedule is that a haphazard or random use of such agents as The Spoiler has been found to lead to more lasting behavior change than a continuous one-to-one application. In addition, of course, by changing the schedule in this way you are beginning to "wean" your Self from using this device.

Continue to wear the rubber band until about one month has passed without your having had any strong impulses to smoke. Return to using The Spoiler any time in the future that you feel the need for some quick and effective help. During those times use it just as you did during the first two weeks.

2. Continue to inscribe "I.Q." on your thumb for at least one more month.

3. Continue doing your daily physical exercises.

4. It is your decision as to how long you want to continue to save money in the "Health Bank" for each cigarette not smoked. It can be anywhere from another week or so to more than a year, but be sure not to forget about it—it is an important positive reinforcement for your Self and should be spent in a way that pleases you. And . . .

> PRACTICE WHAT YOU'VE LEARNED.
> SLOW OR NO PROGRESS WITHOUT IT.

6

Postgraduate

In this chapter you will learn of the three-stage process for *staying stopped,* for remaining a nonsmoker permanently. As you move from one stage to the next you will be strengthening the healthiest parts of your Self while eliminating the last vestiges of the R.S. within you. You will be providing yourself with the strongest basis for becoming a lifelong nonsmoker that I know of when you have moved well into the third stage. The material presented here should raise your level of awareness about the issues underlying cigarette smoking. I hope it will raise your hackles as well.

Never Again: The Three Stages to Staying Stopped

A bit of news for those of you don't know it already: there is no such thing as an absolute guarantee that you will never choose to smoke again. Notice that I said never "choose" to smoke again. Whether or not you smoke again will continue to depend upon a renewable decision which only you can make and which you cannot avoid making. No program, for instance, no matter how powerful it is, can

149

entirely eliminate your capacity to choose to make use of some clever rationalization at some future date in order to begin smoking again. The ultimate responsibility for not smoking, therefore, must always be yours alone.

All of us have heard stories of people who have returned to smoking after being nonsmokers for varying periods of time. Perhaps you were even one of those people. The number of people who return to smoking after having quit is disturbingly high, though it is certainly true that the longer you don't smoke the less likely it is that you will ever return to it.

But *staying stopped* is what it is all about, and the material in this chapter, both directly and indirectly, has precisely that concern as its focus. Everything in this book is included for its practical purpose, helping you along your path to your goal: becoming a *permanent* nonsmoker.

Let's have a talk.

*

YOU, THE READER: I understand that I alone have the responsibility for not returning to smoking, but that isn't much comfort to me. Isn't there an additional method or technique that I can use that will stack the cards more heavily in my favor? Is there something more than just continuing to use the techniques described in the earlier chapters?

DAVID L. GEISINGER: If you've been diligent and careful in your use of the program thus far, you've already made it substantially less likely that you will ever choose to return to smoking in the future. But there is still more that you can do, that you ought to do, if you are seriously concerned with staying stopped forever.

YTR: Serious? Of course I'm serious. I didn't come this far and put in all this time and effort for nothing, did I? I wouldn't want to have to do it all over again. Frankly, it's been a drag kicking this habit—a lot of work, boring and irritating work enough of the time.

DLG: I know how you're feeling—I've been there myself. But some people don't quite do what is needed in order to stop permanently. They may convince themselves that they've gotten free of the *habit* when all they've actually done has been to eliminate the behavior of smoking for a time. The addictive habit usually has deeper roots which can and often do lead to a return to smoking if you don't do something about them. That's why I asked if you were serious. It's my way of asking if you're willing to go the distance, to move on to the next stage. It means a bit more work.

YTR: How much more? I want to know before I sign up for it.

DLG: I wish I could tell you exactly, but I can't. It's an individual matter—it depends on how powerful your habit was, on how many previous attempts at breaking it you've made, on what your own personal resources are, on how much support you have, and the like. My advice to you is to take it all the way. Go as far as you can with the program.

YTR: Is this trip really necessary? Sounds like "overkill" to me.

DLG: That's not the way I think of it. It's insurance for the future.

YTR: Oh, so you're an insurance salesman too?

DLG: Sure, if that's what it takes. At these prices . . .

YTR: O.K., O.K. What do I have to do?

DLG: Well, the first step is to educate yourself.

YRT: Educate myself? About what?

DLG: About the politics of smoking.

YTR: I don't understand. What does politics have to do with smoking?

DLG: Practically everything.

YTR: I still don't get it. What do you mean by politics, and how does it relate to smoking?

DLG: By politics I'm referring to the wheeling and dealing that goes on behind the scenes among the various organizations which have an interest in inducing more and more people to become cigarette smokers, in perpetuating the habit of cigarette smoking among the general population.

YTR: Why would any organization other than cigarette manufacturers have such an interest?

DLG: As you've been reading this book you've already seen that the advertising industry, to take just one example, is fundamentally connected to creating and enhancing the market for cigarettes.

YTR: Sure. It's easy to see that the ad agencies and the cigarette manufacturers work together and mutually benefit each other. The more people are persuaded to smoke, the more cigarettes are sold, the more money is made, and the happier they both are. But that's pretty obvious stuff and no surprise to anyone. You mentioned "various organizations" before. Are there others involved?

DLG: Of course, many others: organizations with great power, talent, and money at their disposal, organizations which are kept going either wholly or partially, either directly or indirectly, from the sales of cigarettes.

YTR: For instance?

DLG: For instance, the press. Since the government prohibited advertising on the airwaves, the principal advertising for cigarettes has appeared in newspapers and magazines. Enormous revenues flow to the written media from the tobacco companies. Since most newspapers and magazines depend very heavily upon advertising dollars, the tobacco interests must have some power and influence over what gets printed in any publication that also prints cigarette ads.

YTR: You can't mean that the tobacco interests determine the policies of the press? I find that difficult to believe. Aren't you getting a little paranoid?

DLG: Well, as someone once said, "Even paranoids have enemies." I mean only that any publication which derives a substantial part of its income from cigarette advertising can't possibly be neutral and objective about smoking and health. Somewhere down the line their self-interest is very likely to come into conflict with the public interest, and then they might be forced to take a stand. Magazines such as *The New Yorker* and *Reader's Digest* have recognized this fact and no longer carry cigarette advertising, but they, obviously, are very much the exceptions in this area.

YTR: But the newspaper I read often runs articles on the dangers of smoking. It doesn't seem to me that they've been biased by the fact that they also carry cigarette ads.

DLG: I don't think that you're examining the issues deeply enough. Of course, if a newspaper carries ads promoting the sale of cigarettes while it also publishes articles of fact on the harm caused by smoking, the very least you can say is that the publication is a bit hypocritical.

YTR: That's not hypocrisy. A newspaper accepts advertising in order to support itself so that it can continue delivering the news to the people. The people have to decide for themselves whether or not to follow the ads. Publishing ads is a morally neutral business. I don't see the hypocrisy in it.

DLG: Let me see if I can clarify things. An ad for cigarettes is not the same as, for instance, an ad for canned peaches. Cigarette smoking causes unmistakable harm to the smoker, to others around the smoker, to the environment. Advertising has one central purpose: to influence, to sell. Make no mistake about it, advertising *does* influence; it works. Therefore, to publish an ad which you know is going to influence a certain number of readers to use a product you know to be harmful is *not* a neutral act; it is a commitment to a point of view. Publications can't hide behind a screen of alleged neutrality in this case. If they're not part of the solution, they're part of the problem.

YTR: Pretty convincing stuff. So the press is implicated and not neutral after all.

DLG: Right. Any publication that makes money from cigarette advertising is necessarily biased in that regard. "Neutrality" supports the status quo. Now, suppose that the government decided to consider passing a law banning the advertising of cigarettes in the printed media just as they banned it on radio and T.V. Do you think the general editorial policy of these publications with regard to such a law would tend to be neutral and unbiased, would reflect an impartial examination of the issues? In most cases this would be a very difficult decision, though some publications, I'm sure, would lend their support, would have the courage to do what is right even though their advertising revenues would suffer for a time.

YTR: I'm beginning to see what you mean. The same bias would probably hold for the people who own the billboards where cigarette ads appear. But who else is implicated, who else benefits from the sale of cigarettes?

DLG: The tobacco farmers are another beneficiary, and they are benefited in at least two ways. In the first place they make money from the sale of their crop to the manufacturers, and in the second place they receive millions of dollars from the U.S. Department of Agriculture in the form of subsidies, price supports, money for tobacco-growing research, and the like.

YTR: But that's sheer madness. The government, through the 1964 Surgeon General's report on smoking and health, has clearly recognized that smoking is definitely dangerous to the health. Why then would it subsidize tobacco farmers?

DLG: Madness it may be, but it exists nevertheless. The government supports the tobacco farmers for the same reason that the press accepts advertising from cigarette companies: money. The revenues from the taxes on tobacco products are enormous, and tobacco taxes are relatively easy to levy. There isn't much protest because only the smokers have to pay the tax, and they're hooked and happy to pay for their "fix" just as long as they can continue to have it. The government, by supporting tobacco interests, is generating money for itself. *Cigarette smoking is in fact a government-supported addiction.* At any rate, the government seems to presume that money is generated in this way.

YTR: Why do you use the word "presume"?

DLG: Because it is a very shortsighted policy for the government to be involved in the furtherance of the tobacco industry in any way, a form of profit-motive myopia. In the long run, cigarette smoking actually *costs* the government a great deal of money, causes a net deficit to the budget. Just consider the astronomical amount of money spent on smoking-related illnesses, add that figure to the cost of the countless hours of work lost in the labor force because of these same illnesses, and the resulting reduction in goods and services produced; add to that such things as the sums given in support of scientific research on these illnesses, and the cost of the thousands of fires started each year by careless smokers, and the costs of educating the people to the dangers of smoking (if that isn't an example of the most absurd hypocrisy, I don't know what is!) and you can see how fiscally irresponsible it is for the government to lend any support whatsoever to the tobacco industry. All the taxpayers, not just smokers, pay for this colossal waste.

YTR: I'm beginning to see the picture, and, of course, the waste is really much greater than you've outlined, the policies more shortsighted than you've suggested. There are costs that can't be measured in dollars alone: no price can be put on the human suffering or on the damage to the environment caused by cigarette smoking. The land that grows tobacco must be very fertile—crops could be grown on it to feed the hungry. Forests that have taken hundreds of years to grow are wiped out in one day from fires started by careless smokers.

DLG: Now you're getting it. The government, the cigarette manufacturers, the advertising agencies, the press, the tobacco growers, are all scratching each other's backs in one way or another. The citizen, smoker and nonsmoker alike, is at the bottom of the heap, in some measure an unsuspecting victim of this unholy alliance. The citizen alone pays these costs with her or his dollars and health.

YTR: But surely there are people in government who are aware of all this. If what you say is true, why hasn't something been done to change these policies? After all, the government is supposed to be of the people, by the people, and for the people. If cigarette smoking is so harmful, is *against* the people, why doesn't the government take the kind of action needed to regulate it more stringently? Is it just because it doesn't want to give up the money it makes from cigarette taxes? Is the federal government trading people's health for money?

DLG: I suppose you could say that, in one sense.

YTR: Come on now—you're being overly cynical.

DLG: Sure I'm a bit of a cynic. It's hard not to be when you examine the situation. First, consider that the federal government is composed of the executive, judiciary, and legislative branches, and remember that laws are drafted primarily by committees in Congress, the legislative branch. These committees are composed of people elected by voters in their particular states to represent their interests. These representatives are therefore not impartial, even on matters where impartiality is truly called for; they are obliged, if they care about getting reelected, to be responsive primarily to the interests of their particular constituency even when those interests go against the larger public's welfare. It is simply extremely naive of anyone to expect these representatives to side with the interests of the larger public in matters that conflict with the interests of the voters in their states. And that isn't the full answer to your question. There's a lot more going on behind the scenes.

YTR: There always is. What else are you referring to?

DLG: To the pressures exerted on members of the Congress by the special-interest groups called lobbies. The wealthier the special-interest group is, the more powerful the pressure it can exert, and the more influential it can be with the lawmakers. The tobacco lobby, as you can well imagine, is an especially powerful and wealthy one.

YTR: Exactly what is the tobacco lobby and how does it fit into the picture?

DLG: It is composed of a group of people in an organization headquartered in Washington, D. C., called the Tobacco Institute. They are funded by and represent the specific interests of the major cigarette manufacturers. They focus their attention on the legislators who sit on committees dealing with tobacco regulations. In the Senate and the House of Representatives about one-third or more of all the committees and subcommittees are chaired or con-trolled by congressmen from the six major tobacco-growing states: Georgia, North Carolina, Kentucky, Vir-ginia, South Carolina, and Tennessee.[1] This means, of course, that the government's policies on tobacco are set, in effect, by these special-interest groups, and they are obviously not especially interested in promoting public health if it means a decline in cigarette sales. There have been a number of bills introduced over the years that would have restricted the tobacco industry by eliminating the federal tobacco subsidy but they got nowhere; they died in committee.

YTR: That doesn't mean that nothing can be done about it. The situation isn't really hopeless, is it?

DLG: Not at all. The number of people who want to bring about a change in these policies is growing more rapidly than ever. Antismoking groups are organizing throughout the country and gaining power; they are beginning to bring about changes in the laws on a local level. Nonsmokers are becoming aware that they have rights too, and *the right to breathe clean air must always take precedence over the right of others to smoke when there is a conflict between the two.* You may do what you like with your health, but you have no right to interfere with mine. I believe that we are on the verge of a great change in this country and the change is beginning, as it must, on a grass-roots level. If it keeps growing the way it has been, Congress will be forced to respond.

1. Sidney S. Field, "Time to Crack the Tobacco Lobby," *Reader's Digest,* July 1976.

YTR: I think you have a point there, but now you're being naive. The government won't be able to stop people from smoking; just look at the failure of prohibition in the 1920s. If people want to smoke, they'll smoke.

DLG: Of course; the government shouldn't be in the business of telling people how to live their private lives anyhow. But that isn't the point. The government should be involved in this matter, but in a limited way: first, it should stop subsidizing the tobacco industry entirely; second, it should support by law the rights of nonsmokers as having precedence over the rights of smokers in public places, if for no other reason than that a very large majority of the people are nonsmokers (about 75 percent of the population does not smoke); third, it should severely restrict *all* public advertising of cigarettes (kids as well as adults are being influenced by the ads they see); and fourth, it should be engaged in a massive and continuing effort to educate the public to the dangers of smoking, and the costs of this campaign should be paid for by money collected from cigarette taxes.

YRT: Do you really think that if the government took the steps you suggested cigarette smoking would be eliminated? I think that you're still being naive; some people will always smoke—the Native Americans smoked long before cigarette manufacturers, advertising, the press, and the government got into the act.

DLG: I have no doubt that a substantial number of people would still smoke even if all the suggestions I just made were carried out. Moreover, as I said before, I don't think the government ought to be in the business of telling people whether they can or cannot smoke—only in protecting the rights of nonsmokers. I think it is very likely that after some years these new policies would result in a very dramatic decline in the number of smokers in the United States. When the government was in high gear on its antismoking campaign in the late 1960s the incidence of cigarette smoking dropped significantly. Once again advertising proved effective, this time by the government. But when the government banned cigarette ads from the airwaves, in 1971, the tobacco industry redirected its energies. It bombarded the printed media with a tremendous number of ads and flooded the market with one new cigarette after another. Pretty soon it had erased the gains made by the antismoking campaign.

As for the Native Americans, although they smoked, they did so on special occasions in a limited, ritualized way, and they didn't smoke cigarettes. In any event, smoking was a very different matter in their culture until tobacco became an item of exchange with the white person's culture. As soon as someone found a way to make a profit from tobacco, the race was on to promote the product. It is a race which has been picking up speed ever since, a race which has gotten entirely out of control.

YTR: You know, David, this discussion is pretty interesting and informative but frankly I don't see what bearing it has on my personal smoking problem. It may seem self-centered, but I'm primarily interested in my own welfare at this time and in this situation. I want to remain a nonsmoker, to have kicked the damned habit once and for all, and that's all I really care about. Earlier you said that the material in this chapter had a practical aim, but I don't get the practical significance of what we've been talking about. How is it going to help me to know all this stuff?

DLG: Good question. What it boils down to is this: if you care as much as you say you do about *remaining* a nonsmoker, the most effective way of assuring that you reach your goal is to increase your commitment to it. What I mean by this is really quite simple. The more deeply you consider these facts, review them, think about their ramifications and consequences, the more you see how as a smoker you personally were seduced into becoming an addict by a system created to benefit the tobacco interests at the expense of your health, the greater will be your commitment to remaining a non-smoker; and, as I said before, the strength of your commitment is directly related to the success you'll have in reaching your goal. Also, the more positive habits you develop, such as physical exercise and unmasking, the more committed you will be to remaining a nonsmoker.

YTR: Are you saying that all I need to do is to educate myself and I'll remain a nonsmoker?

DLG: Not entirely. There are no guarantees, remember? Education accompanied by a *personal* consideration of the material is just the first step of a three-step process of deepening commitment. It is what might be called the thinking or information-gathering stage. If you've taken the time to educate yourself in this way, you've begun to stack the cards in favor of making your status as a nonsmoker a permanent one. You've improved your chances considerably over those of people who stop smoking without moving up to this stage.

YTR: You mentioned three steps. What's the next one?

DLG: The next step is a by-product of the first one. It leads to a stage in which your *feelings* become activated by the information you learned earlier, a stage where the emotional component comes into play. While you are continuing to reflect on the information contained in this book, learning all you can about the issues involved, keeping your eyes open to articles in the newspapers and magazines on the subject of smoking—they appear quite regularly—begin to work on bringing it down to a personal, *gut* level.

YTR: That's easier said than done. How do I manage to do that?

DLG: By continually asking yourself the question, "How does or did this affect or concern *me*?" you must actively put yourself in the picture every chance you get. You were a smoker, you were "had," and your parents, relatives, and friends who smoke have been "had," and people you knew or heard about, who got sick or died from one of the diseases caused by cigarette smoking, were "had." If you have children or are planning on having children, they stand a good chance of being "had" in the same way. How does this knowledge make you feel?

YTR: Well, when you put it that way it makes me feel angry. In fact, the more I think about it the angrier I feel.

DLG: Exactly. Anger is the feeling most people experience when they come to realize how they've been taken in, how they've been duped. But it's easy to feel temporarily annoyed, indignant, even outraged, when it begins to dawn on you that there was a lot more to the matter of your cigarette smoking than you had ever considered. The important thing is to stay aware of these feelings, to keep them alive, refreshing them from time to time by learning all you can about the issues discussed here. Each time you see an article or an ad relating to smoking you might spend a moment thinking about it; personalize it, bring it back home.

YTR: Sounds like more work. Why bother? What's the payoff?

DLG: As always, whatever bother is involved will prove to be for the most practical of reasons and will be well worth it. To do something well usually takes practice or repetition and that *is* work. It requires some discipline and effort, of course, but the greater effort you put into this, the more you get out of it. Since you care about never returning to the habit, your effort will be more than repaid.

Let's not get overly dramatic though. It really isn't that much work at this stage. Don't forget about all the benefits and good feelings you have been deriving and will continue to derive from kicking the habit: the benefits to your physical health—the increased energy and stamina you are developing, the years you are adding to your life—and the psychological benefits as well—the enhancement of your self-concept, a sense of pride in yourself, of liking yourself better, a sense that comes from knowing that you have what it takes to liberate yourself from the bondage of a habit that could kill you. It is a significant boost to your morale to have stopped smoking, a boost that can help motivate you to take on other projects for self-improvement more successfully, should you desire to do so.

The purpose of remaining aware of your feelings in these matters is twofold: in the first place, these feelings are an effective barrier against becoming reinfluenced by slippery rationalizations about smoking, and in the second place, these feelings provide the natural lead-in to the third and last step in this process of strengthening your commitment to lifelong nonsmoking.

YTR: But what am I supposed to do with the information I'm acquiring? What am I supposed to do with my anger now that I've become aware of it?

DLG: "Do" is the key word here. The third step is that of *action*. It brings you to the stage during which you are making use of what you've learned and felt in order to take a stand, to make your feelings or your position known to others. Action is the sincerest and most effective form of commitment. You may choose to take a limited action for entirely personal reasons—it is O.K. to be quite self-centered in your actions concerning smoking, to act out of a sense of self-protection without trying to get others to agree with your point of view—or you may wish to take a broader political stand, one which is designed to bring about a change in public policy. You may choose to do both, of course. In any case, you'll have moved along the path necessary for permanent change, the path that stretches from thinking to feeling to acting.

YTR: What specific kinds of action do you have in mind?

DLG: Well, let's begin with the personal level. I have a feeling that you may already have taken action in this area. For instance, getting rid of ashtrays in your home or office, sitting in the nonsmoking sections of public places, asking people who are letting the smoke from their cigarettes drift into your face kindly to stop doing so, asking people not to smoke in your home. Incidentally, many people have begun putting small signs on their front doors saying something like, "Thank you for not smoking in our home," or, "Please smoke outside." Try it; it will save you the trouble of having to repeat it to visitors who smoke. Even the "I. Q." that you print on your thumb each day is the kind of personal act that I'm referring to. Keep doing it for another month or two. Invent your own actions as well, ones that make the most sense to you, that you personally find most useful or relevant.

At the beginning of this chapter when I indicated that there were no absolute guarantees that could be made about remaining a nonsmoker, I meant it quite literally. But I *can* offer you something which in my judgment is as close to such a guarantee as it is humanly possible to get. Whether you choose to go that far is wholly up to you.

YTR: Let's hear about it. I'm not sure I'll need it, but I guess that the more options I have the better. What do I have to do, sew my lips shut?

DLG: Nothing that drastic. What I'm referring to is more of the same: intensifying your commitment by making the move to the most advanced level of this last stage, the level of public action. Once you've become involved in changing public policy, you've gone about as far as you can go. You can work on either the local or national level. For instance, you can circulate a petition to ban all public advertising of cigarettes in your community (billboards are an especially important target), or a petition to require that all public places have separate sections reserved for nonsmokers, or, depending upon how you feel about this issue, that public places such as movie theaters ban smoking entirely. Write your congressional representatives and ask them to support legislation to end the government's subsidies to the tobacco industry; ask your elected officials to get behind a drive to spend more money on antismoking campaigns, on public education about cigarette smoking and health. You can also join existing organizations such as GASP and ASH [addresses given in Chapter 2]. In their literature and newsletters you'll learn how you can lend your support to ongoing efforts in this area. There is an enormous amount to be done—you can be as inventive as your imagination will reach.

In Berkeley I noticed a huge billboard advertising the cigarette Decade (decadence), one of the latest disasters to be loosed on the public by the tobacco companies. Someone had eliminated the "C" and the second "E" in the name. Pretty effective advertising, I'd say, and a move in the right direction.

But it sure would be fine if there were no longer

billboards advertising cigarettes, if the ban on cigarette advertising extended to all the printed media as well. It sure would be fine if, instead of 55 million Americans who smoked, there were perhaps only 5 million or less within two generations after these changes in public policy were implemented. It sure would be fine if we could look forward to a future, in a generation or two, where lung cancer and emphysema and heart disease were becoming relatively rare, where tobacco lands were growing food crops instead, where the billions of dollars consumed and wasted by the direct and indirect costs of cigarette smoking were put to uses that would benefit life on the planet, where our children and their children were no longer being persuaded to bring harm to themselves. It sure would be fine if we finally stopped passing on our deadly habits to future generations as part of their heritage. It sure would be fine if we got started NOW.

*

And there, dear reader, you have it. The rest is up to you. Please don't hesitate to refer back to any part of the book for a refresher course when and if you need it.

When I stopped smoking, I had an occasional urge for a cigarette as long as two or three years after "Q" day, but the urges became fewer and weaker as time passed and were easier and easier to beat. I think most ex-smokers have similar experiences, so don't feel discouraged if this should happen to you.

For many of you the most difficult part of becoming an ex-smoker has already come and gone; for others it may be a somewhat longer struggle, but in a very real sense it is a struggle for life itself. It is worth the effort. Stick with it.

Remember, cigarettes are exceptionally addictive to people who were once smokers: even one drag will exert a surprisingly powerful "pull" on you to return to smoking. Don't gamble with smoking. Your life is at stake.

Stay alive to staying alive.

Pitfall

Not smoking is an ongoing process. "I've got it licked" is the most common game played by people who return to smoking. The most important pitfall at this stage is that you will not take the program as far as you need to. Don't make this mistake.

Keep at it. Go the distance.

Exercise

This is the last exercise and the coda to the program. Following, in the next chapter, are some facts and data which have been arranged into a number of categories. Read them at your leisure. Reflect on them and allow their impact to stir your feelings. Use them to fuel your actions, and . . .

PRACTICE WHAT YOU'VE LEARNED.
SLOW OR NO PROGRESS WITHOUT IT.

7

♊

Professorship

You are about to enter the land of facts, figures, and reasonable speculations. Some of you will be comfortable with such matters as statistics and medical information and some of you won't. Nevertheless, this chapter *is not optional*—it is an integral part of the program. Read the following material slowly and carefully, and reflect on the significance of what you are reading. Read with emotional understanding—with your heart—not just with your eyes and your intellect. Take it in.

Remember, what follows is only a small sample from the vast amount of information against smoking—a drop in the proverbial bucket.

- How much do you need?
- How much does anyone need?
- How much does any government need?
- How much does the world need?

Cancer

Cigarette smoking is *the* major cause of lung cancer.[1]

1. *San Francisco Chronicle* (UPI), June 29, 1974.

Cancer of the larynx, oral cavity, esophagus, urinary bladder, kidney, and pancreas have all been linked to cigarette smoking.[2] For instance, cigarette smoking causes half of all bladder cancers in men and one-third of such cancers in women.[3]

The lung cancer rate among people who never smoked is 12.8 per 100,000; among people who smoke less than half a pack a day it is 95.2 per 100,000; among people who smoke one-half to one pack a day it is 107.8 per 100,000; among one- to two-pack-a-day smokers it is 229.2 per 100,000; among people who smoke more than two packs a day it is 264.2 per 100,000.[4]

The total number of Americans who died of cigarette-induced lung cancer within the first six years after the *Surgeon General's Report on Smoking and Health* (1964) is approximately ten times as great as the number of deaths caused by dropping the A-bomb on Hiroshima.[5]

In the mid-1970s in the United States alone, about 84,000 people die each year from lung cancer whereas only about 3000 died from lung cancer in 1930.[6] Ninety-five percent of all lung cancer victims are heavy smokers.[7]

Deaths from lung cancer among women increased 400 percent since 1930, and, as one might predict, the percentage

2. U. S. Department of Health, Education and Welfare, *Surgeon General's Report on Smoking and Health,* 1971.
3. *San Francisco Chronicle* (AP), September 29, 1977.
4. *Changing Times* Magazine, March 1962.
5. T. Whiteside, *Selling Death; Cigarette Advertising and Public Health* (New York: Liveright, 1971).
6. Sidney S. Field, "Time to Crack the Cigarette Lobby," *Reader's Digest,* July 1976.
7. *San Francisco Sunday Examiner and San Francisco Chronicle,* May 2, 1976.

of women who smoke increased 350 percent during that same period.[8] This is no coincidence. The lung cancer rate among women has doubled in the past ten years alone.[9]

Nicotine—and possibly cancer-causing substances as well—collects in the breast fluids of women smokers, whether or not they are nursing.[10] Breast cancer is increasing at the rate of 1 percent a year [11]

Emphysema and Chronic Bronchitis

According to the 1971 *Surgeon General's Report on Smoking and Health*, cigarette smoking is *the* most important cause of chronic obstructive broncho-pulmonary disease in the United States.[12] Chronic bronchitis and emphysema, the major diseases in this category, kill about 25,000 persons in the United States each year.[13]

The death rate from these diseases is 500 percent greater for smokers than for nonsmokers.[14]

Deaths from emphysema, primarily a smoker's disease, have increased 100 percent in the past 15 years.[15]

8. See footnote 2 above.
9. *Consumer Reports,* May 1976.
10. *San Francisco Chronicle,* January 12, 1978.
11. *San Francisco Chronicle,* October 22, 1976.
12. See footnote 2 above.
13. See footnote 1 above.
14. See footnote 2 above.
15. See footnote 6 above.

Miscellaneous Health Issues

Dr. Thomas J. Mulvaney of Harvard Medical School describes cigarette smoking as the "single greatest preventable health hazard in the world."[16]

Smoking radically increases the pulse rate and raises the blood pressure.[17] Heart and blood diseases are the leading causes of death in the United States. The death rate from these diseases is twice as high among smokers as among nonsmokers.[18]

"Sidestream" smoke (smoke going directly into the air from the lit end of the cigarette) contains even higher concentrations of poisons than "mainstream" smoke (smoke drawn in through the cigarette itself). It has two times as much tar and nicotine, three times as much benzpyrene, five times as much carbon monoxide, fifty times as much ammonia, and more cadmium.[19] Cigarette smoke contains one million times more particles of benzpyrene (one of its many cancer-producing substances) than polluted air.[20]

The concentration of hydrogen cyanide—the deadly gas used in gas chambers—in cigarette smoke is 1600 parts per million (ppm), but long-term exposure to levels above only 10 ppm is considered dangerous. A nitrogen dioxide level of 5 ppm

16. *Harvard Magazine,* March 1976.
17. *San Francisco Bay Guardian,* May 31, 1975.
18. See footnote 6 above.
19. See footnote 16 above.
20. A. Brody and B. Brody, *The Legal Rights of Non-Smokers* (New York: Avon Books, 1977).

in the air is considered dangerous. It is found in 250 ppm in cigarette smoke.[21]

According to Dr. Nicholas Ward of Oxford University, filter tips pass on *more* carbon monoxide than nonfilters do, and this has been linked to heart ailments.[22] It takes hours for the carbon monoxide to leave the body; after three to four hours, half the excess carbon monoxide is still in the bloodstream.[23] Researchers say that nearly half of all nonsmoking Americans have dangerous levels of carbon monoxide in their blood, and tobacco smoking was the single most important factor responsible. Smokers had three times or more the amount of carbon monoxide in their blood as nonsmokers did.[24]

A nonsmoker breathes in the equivalent of one cigarette when in a closed room in which ten cigarettes are smoked.[25]

The American Medical Association estimates that 34 million people are allergic or sensitive to cigarette smoke.[26]

An average pack-a-day smoker inhales more than one-half cup of tar each year.[27]

The burning tip of the cigarette, as it is drawn, reaches 1600 degrees Fahrenheit.[28]

21. American Lung Association, *Second Hand Smoke* (pamphlet).
22. See footnote 7 above.
23. See footnote 21 above.
24. *San Francisco Chronicle* (AP), August 27, 1974.
25. *San Francisco Sunday Examiner* and *San Francisco Chronicle, Atlas World Press Review,* April 18, 1976
26. See footnote 17 above.
27. W. S. Ross, "Poison Gases in Your Cigarettes—Part II," *Reader's Digest,* December 1976.
28. *San Francisco Examiner,* February 4, 1978.

Women who take birth control pills and who smoke are three times more likely to die of a heart attack than nonsmokers on the pill.[29]

Women who smoke are likely to undergo menopause at a younger age than nonsmokers.[30]

Smoking wrinkles the skin of the face.[31]

Mortality rates from gastric and duodenal ulcers are very much higher among cigarette smokers than among nonsmokers.[32]

Fifty-six percent of fatal residential fires are the result of smoking.[33]

Cigarette smoking also slows down the rate of ulcer healing.[34]

Smokers have about twice as many auto accidents as nonsmokers.[35]

Chronic smoking may inhibit sexual performance.[36]

In a study of 32,000 people, male smokers under 45 spent 71 percent more time in the hospital than nonsmokers.[37]

29. *San Francisco Chronicle* (AP), April 3, 1978.
30. *San Francisco Chronicle (The New York Times),* July 7, 1977.
31. *San Francisco Chronicle,* August 6, 1977.
32. See footnote 4 above.
33. See footnote 20 above.
34. See footnote 17 above.
35. See footnote 20 above.
36. *Today's Health* Magazine, August 1974.
37. *San Francisco Sunday Examiner* and *San Francisco Chronicle, Atlas World Press Review,* July 31, 1977.

Approximately one-sixth (about 300,000) of the annual deaths from all causes in the United States are smoking-related.[38]

Effects of Smoking on Infants and Children

Two-thirds of the children in the United States reside with at least one smoker.[39] The children of smokers become ill much more frequently than those of nonsmokers, usually from respiratory diseases; these children also tend to have higher blood pressure and pulse rates.[40]

The incidence of bronchitis and pneumonia in the first year of life is lowest where neither parent smokes, highest where both smoke, and in the middle where only one smokes.[41]

In twenty homes of asthmatic children where smoking had been eliminated, eighteen children showed an improvement in health.[42]

Cigarette smoking causes a retarding influence on fetal growth and causes a higher stillbirth and neonatal death rate.[43]

The babies of heavy-smoking fathers had about twice the expected incidence of severe malformations, in one study. There is also an increased perinatal mortality rate where the father-to-be smoked about one pack of cigarettes a day.[44]

38. See footnote 20 above.
39. See footnote 20 above.
40. See footnote 17 above.
41. See footnote 20 above.
42. See footnote 20 above.
43. See footnote 17 above.
44. See footnote 20 above.

For seven hours after a pregnant woman smokes only one cigarette, the carbon monoxide level in maternal and fetal blood increases 10 percent and the oxygen supply to the infant is thereby decreased.[45]

It has been estimated that a pregnant woman who is a smoker runs as much as a 30 percent greater risk of losing her child than does a nonsmoking woman.[46]

Demography and General Statistics

More than 3.5 *trillion* cigarettes were smoked around the world in 1975, a gain of almost 1 trillion over the 1960–1964 yearly average.[47]

America's cigarette production in 1976 will reach an estimated 700 billion, of which 62 billion were for export.[48]

Twenty-six low tar brands of cigarettes were introduced in 1977 alone.[49] In the mid-1950s there were only sixteen brands of cigarettes; now there are about one hundred and fifty.[50]

Antismoking campaigns in England have been most successful among male teachers and professional men, where smoking has been virtually halved in the past 15 years. Although there is a clear overall decline in cigarette smoking

45. See footnote 20 above.
46. See footnote 20 above.
47. See footnote 3 above.
48. *Rocky Mountain News,* January 4, 1977.
49. *Wall Street Journal,* March 21, 1978.
50. *San Francisco Chronicle (The New York Times),* November 12, 1976.

in Britain, the number of female factory workers who smoke actually increased by 6 percent over the past 15 years.[51]

Older men are giving up cigarette smoking in significantly larger numbers. From 1968 to 1972 the heart attack rate for white men between the ages of 35 and 64 years dropped nearly 9 percent. According to Dr. J. Stamler, "The biggest single factor, in my judgement, in the downturn of premature heart attacks is the change of cigarette smoking patterns."[52]

In the United States the proportion of cigarette smokers among adults has fallen from 53 percent in 1964 to 39 percent 1975. Among women, the proportion of smokers fell from 34 percent in 1966 to 29 percent in 1975.[53]

In Japan, 70 percent of the men smoke while only 9 percent of the women do.[54] So far.

Statisticians say that there are 6,000,000 smokers between the ages of 13 and 19.[55] It has been estimated that 4000 teenagers take up smoking each day in the United States, and that continuing that rate would lead to 1,000,000 youngsters now in school dying of lung cancer before they reached the age of 70.[56]

51. *San Francisco Sunday Examiner* and *San Francisco Chronicle* (Reuters), January 15, 1978.
52. *San Francisco Chronicle,* January 24, 1975.
53. E. Eckholm, "The Unnatural History of Tobacco," *Natural History Magazine,* April 1977.
54. See footnote 53 above.
55. See footnote 10 above.
56. A. L. Fritschler, *Smoking and Politics: Policymaking and the Federal Bureaucracy* (Englewood Cliffs, N.J.: Prentice-Hall, 1975).

Smoking among teenage females has doubled in the past ten years.[57] Thirty percent of boys of school age smoke; 27 percent of girls of school age smoke.[58]

The butts and wrappers of the 80 million packs of cigarettes smoked daily add up to 1760 tons of trash.[59]

American smokers send nearly 40 tons of solid air pollution, in the form of smoke particles, into the skies each day.[60]

Advertising

An estimated $500 million a year is spent on cigarette advertising.[61]

In 1971 the tobacco companies spent over 1000 percent more money on billboard advertising than they did just before the 1971 ban on cigarette ads over the airwaves.[62]

About $40 million was spent on advertising of Merit cigarettes alone during the year the brand was introduced.[63] The manufacturers can afford these astronomical expenditures because a mere 1 percent of the market means sales of $75 million.[64]

Twenty-five million sample packs of Real cigarettes were distributed free on street corners all over the country.[65]

57. See footnote 31 above.
58. See footnote 11 above.
59. See footnote 16 above.
60. See footnote 16 above.
61. *San Francisco Chronicle,* February 27, 1978.
62. See footnote 5 above.
63. *Business Week,* December 6, 1976.
64. *San Francisco Sunday Examiner* and *San Francisco Chronicle,* May 30, 1976.
65. See footnote 49 above.

Thirty thousand VWs are driving around painted with ad displays for Kool.[66]

The American Cancer Society said that women and blacks have been the special targets of cigarette ads.[67] ASH director Paul Hodges says that tobacco ads are consistently aiming at working-class people and women.[68] Among white men and women, blue-collar workers outsmoked white-collar workers. Black people, by percentages, smoked more than whites.[69]

Politics and Economics

Eighty-five to one hundred billion dollars a year is spent by consumers around the world on tobacco.[70] In the United States tobacco was a $10 billion consumer product in 1970.[71]

Smokers contribute about $6 billion annually in taxes to federal, state, and local governments.[72] But consider the costs of production losses, medical care, research in smoking and health, property losses from smoking-related fires, property losses from smoking-related accidents, and government subsidies to tobacco interests:

1. Between $11 billion and $18 billion annually in the United States is spent on health and hospital treatment of tobacco-related illness, and approximately 80 million lost work days annually can be attributed to the effects of cigarette smoking.[73]

---

66. See footnote 49 above.
67. *San Francisco Chronicle,* June 5, 1975.
68. See footnote 51 above.
69. *San Francisco Sunday Examiner* and *San Francisco Chronicle,* October 1, 1977.
70. See footnote 53 above.
71. See footnote 5 above.
72. See footnote 20 above.
73. GASP *Resuscitator* (reprinted from the *Washington Star),* March-April 1978.

2. Smoking employees on the average cost their companies $750 per year because of distraction from work, sick leave, and shortened life span.[74]

3. The federal government provides over $80 million in subsidies to tobacco farmers each year.[75] But the federal government spends only $8 million each year for National Cancer Institute research on the hazardous substances in tobacco and cigarette smoke.[76]

The new HEW program calls for a budget of only $6 million to discourage smoking, although the Secretary of HEW, Dr. Joseph Califano, calls cigarette smoking, "Public health enemy number one."[77]

"To date every legislative attempt to impose federal control on the manufacture of cigarettes has been blocked by members of the tobacco lobby [The Tobacco Institute]. Since 1966, for instance, upwards of 150 bills that would have banned federal tobacco subsidies, or otherwise would have affected the cigarette industry, have been buried in committee."[78]

Three of the top five cigarette producers in the world are public enterprises (China, USSR, Japan). The other two are the British-American Tobacco Company, and Philip Morris, Inc. China has the world's largest tobacco industry.[79] In France, a government monopoly runs the cigarette business.

74. See footnote 17 above.
75. *San Francisco Chronicle* (Newsday), February 1, 1978.
76. See footnote 6 above.
77. See footnote 61 above.
78. See footnote 6 above.
79. See footnote 53 above.

According to the minister of health, the French people are spending more on cigarettes than on bread and fruit.[80]

In the United States, tobacco has been included in Public Law 480, the "Food for Peace" program, which involves agricultural sales to needy countries![81]

"Cigarette smoking is increasing in poor nations because tobacco producers are presenting it as a symbol of progress [!] to third world peoples."[82]

Life Expectancy

Men who smoke two or more packs of cigarettes a day cut their life expectancy 14 to 15 years, and women smokers of two or more packs a day cut their life expectancy by 19 to 20 years.[83]

A cigarette smoker shortens his or her life span by about 5.5 minutes for each cigarette smoked, according to a study by the Royal College of Physicians.[84]

When smokers quit, the excess risk of bladder cancer tends to decline after seven years or longer.[85]

A study of 5000 people showed that men over 65 who gave up cigarette smoking suffered from fewer heart attacks and lived longer than men who continued to smoke.[86]

80. *San Francisco Chronicle,* October 28, 1975.
81. See footnote 53 above.
82. *San Francisco Examiner,* March 19, 1978.
83. *San Francisco Chronicle* (UPI), October 13, 1975.
84.*San Francisco Chronicle* (Reuters), June 2, 1977.
85. See footnote 3 above.
86. *San Francisco Chronicle,* December 29, 1974.

If you stopped smoking ten years ago, your life expectancy equals that of persons who never smoked, according to the National Center for Disease Control.[87]

*

Summing up the most recent trends, it appears that cigarette smoking is most rapidly declining among college-educated, white, middle- and upper-middle-class men, and it seems to be on the rise among blue-collar workers, women, blacks, Third World people, and adolescents, particularly adolescent girls.

This pattern, like all such patterns, is no accident. These groups are precisely the ones who have become the carefully selected targets of the cigarette manufacturers' latest advertising and sales compaigns.

How much more death and destruction has to be marketed to the people before the government will finally take stronger action?

The people must speak, for themselves and their children. For the earth. Louder!

You are one of those people.

---

87. *Oakland Tribune* (AP), May 7, 1977.

Index

185

life expectancy of, 182
organizations of, 14-15
political action by, 158-61,
165-66
progress as, 110-16, 133-36,
145-46
rights of, 14, 53, 106, 130-31,
138-41, 144-45, 158-61,
165-66
statistics, 170, 171, 172, 173,
182
support of and for, 119, 136,
138.
See also Stopping smoking

P

pacifiers, 85-87, 96, 131
Philip Morris, 180
physical exercise, 34, 49, 72, 87-
91, 96, 132, 147, 161
pipe smoking, 138-39
poisonous gases, in cigarettes,
34, 61, 123, 141-42, 172-73
premature aging, smoking
linked to, 78, 174

R

Raleigh, Walter, 17
Reader's Digest, 153
relaxation exercises, 34, 83-85

Reynaud's disease, smoking
linked to, 78
Richmond, Julius, 145
Robot Smoker, 54-57, 63-66, 72,
73, 78-79, 81, 82, 83, 90, 91-
92, 94, 100, 102-3, 109, 112,
114, 134, 135
rationalizations by (RuSes),
116-19, 131, 145-46
Royal College of Physicians,
181
RuSes, of Robot Smoker, 116-
19, 131, 145-46

S

Self, 46, 63-65, 73, 79, 81, 82, 83,
90, 91-92, 94, 99, 100, 103,
112, 134
nurturing and protecting of,
105-7, 109, 114, 118-19,
132, 134, 143-44
smoking (cigarettes):
as addiction, 13, 14, 15, 22,
56, 61, 73-75, 94-95, 143-44
autonomic conditioning in,
73, 77-78
brand indentification in, 54-
56
case histories, 18-19, 25-26
children and, 66, 125, 130,
175-76
as conditioned reflex, 57-60,
107-8

I would greatly appreciate hearing from any of you who have comments about the program described in this book. Information about your results with the program as well as additional ideas and/or suggestions for improvements will be most helpful for subsequent editions. Please write to me in care of the publisher. Thanks.